THE INTUITIVE ENTREPRENEUR

DEEPER CONNECTIONS FOR SOUL-DRIVEN SUCCESS

DEB DECELLE

FEATURING: LISA ATTANASIO : DONNABELLE CASIS : MICHELE CUTLER : BECKY DOTSON

DEBORAH DRUMMOND : JOANNE FIGOV : JAMES O. JOSEPH JR. : KIELA KASOMANY

KAZEMARU : LIZ GOLL LERNER : SHANNON MITCHELL : CARM OSULLIVAN : NICOLE POPE

KRISTIN ROSMORDUC : JILL SEABOURNE : JULIE SPEETJENS : DANA THERESA : BRADFORD W. TILDEN

LÉVONTA WHITE : L'AURA MONTGOMERY WILLIAMS : EMILY ATLANTIS WOLF

THE INTUITIVE ENTREPRENEUR

Deeper Connections for Soul-Driven Success

Deb DeCelle

FEATURING: Lisa Attanasio : Donnabelle Casis : Michele Cutler :
Becky Dotson : Deborah Drummond : Joanne Figov : James O. Joseph Jr. :
Kiela Kasomany : Kazemaru : Liz Goll Lerner : Shannon Mitchell :
Carm OSullivan : Nicole Pope : Kristin Rosmorduc : Jill Seabourne :
Julie Speetjens : Dana Theresa : Bradford W. Tilden
LèVonta White : L'Aura Montgomery Williams : Emily Atlantis Wolf

The Intuitive Entrepreneur
Deeper Connections for Soul-Driven Success
©Copyright 2025 Deb DeCelle
Published by Brave Healer Productions
Paperback ISBN: 978-1-961493-66-7
eBook ISBN: 978-1-961493-67-4

BRAVE HEALER
PUBLISHING
experience what's possible

DISCLAIMER

This book is designed to provide competent, reliable, and educational information regarding business growth, health, wellness, and other subject matter covered. However, it is sold with the understanding the authors and publisher specifically disclaim all responsibility for any liability, loss, or risk, personal or otherwise, incurred as a consequence, directly or indirectly, of the use and application of any of the contents of this publication.

In order to maintain the anonymity of others, the names and identifying characteristics of some people, places, and organizations described in this book have been changed.

This publication contains content that may be potentially triggering or disturbing. Individuals who are sensitive to certain themes are advised to exercise caution while reading.

The opinions, ideas, and recommendations contained in this publication do not necessarily represent those of the Publisher. The use of any information provided in this book is solely at your own risk.

Our authors represent cultures worldwide and as such, there may be differences in language and expressions. As a global publisher, we have made the conscious choice to not edit these nuances so each chapter is authentic and in its author's words.

Know that the experts here have shared their tools, practices, and knowledge with you with a sincere and generous intent to assist you on your business journey. Please contact them with any questions you may have about the techniques or information they provided. They will be happy to assist you further and be an ongoing resource for your success!

DEDICATION

To my husband, Heath, whose unwavering love, support, and belief in my dreams have carried me through every milestone, thank you for standing beside me, cheering me on, and reminding me of my worth.

There truly is no other love like ours.

To my boys, Tim and Matt, whose laughter and curiosity are a constant source of inspiration. You are my greatest joy, my deepest purpose, and my most beautiful adventure. May you always trust the whispers of your hearts and believe in the power of your own brilliant light.

TABLE OF CONTENTS

FOREWORD

There's a moment—when you just know. It's not a maybe. It's not a "let me think about it." It's not even logical. It's a full-body, soul-deep, undeniable YES.

I've built my entire life on that YES.

And the few times I ignored it? Chaos. Every. Single. Time. Because logic will try to keep you safe, but intuition? Intuition will set you free.

I didn't always trust it. For years, I let my mind talk me out of what my soul already knew. I made choices that looked good on paper but felt hollow in my heart. I stayed in places longer than I should have, accepted opportunities that didn't light me up, and silenced my inner knowing in favor of the "smart" choice. And every time I veered off course, life had a way of shaking me up, whispering (or, let's be real, sometimes screaming) for me to listen.

Then one day, I finally did.

I took off on a whirlwind solo journey to Italy for three months - no plan, no safety net, not even the money to justify it, just a deep knowing that I had to go. Every practical reason told me to stay put, to be responsible, to wait until the "right time." But something inside of me refused to be ignored. So I listened.

That trip changed everything. I wrote my bestselling book "Love Yourself Happy" there, but more than that, I rewrote myself. I found the version of me that had been buried under doubt, expectations, and overthinking. I learned what it meant to trust - not just in the universe, but in myself.

I said YES when the world told me no. I trusted when every logical circumstance said, "Are you out of your mind?" And do you know where that got me? In front of millions. On TV. Not by accident, but by alignment. By following that electric, goosebump-giving, soul-expanding pull toward what was already mine.

That's how my TV talk show, Good Morning Joy, was born. Not from a strategy meeting. Not from a perfectly planned roadmap. But from a calling. A knowing. A vision that had no business making sense, yet it did - because it was never supposed to be reasonable. It was supposed to be right.

And that's exactly how I met Deb.

My inbox is a revolving door of opportunities, pitches, and invitations, but I've learned to filter out the noise by tuning into something deeper. And when I met Deb, my intuition didn't whisper - it shouted. I knew, in an instant, that we would work together. There was no second-guessing, no pros-and-cons list, no need to "sleep on it." My gut said yes. Resoundingly, unequivocally, YES.

And here we are.

That's the thing about intuition - it doesn't explain itself. It doesn't beg to be understood. It doesn't care about logic, obstacles, or your well-reasoned excuses. It speaks. And when it does, you have a choice: trust it or regret it.

And that's exactly what this book is about.

Deb DeCelle has gathered the wisdom of intuitive entrepreneurs - trailblazers who didn't wait for permission, proof, or the perfect moment. They didn't need guarantees or blueprints. They followed their knowing. They listened when the whispers of their souls turned into roars. And because of that, they are now leaving behind a roadmap - not for you to follow exactly, but to show you what's possible when you dare to trust yourself.

These aren't just stories. They're proof. Proof that success isn't about formulas - it's about frequency. It's about alignment. It's about the courage to say yes before you know how.

This book is a gift. A guide. A reminder that the greatest business strategy you'll ever have is already inside you. That the biggest opportunities won't come from a spreadsheet, but from a gut feeling. That the life you're dreaming of is already dreaming of you.

And if you listen (really listen), it will take you exactly where you're meant to go.

So take a breath. Tune in. And when your intuition speaks?

Say YES.

Shari Alyse

America's Joy Magnet

- *TV Personality*
- *2x TEDx Speaker*
- *International Bestselling Author*

Iinstagram: @ShariAlyse

TikTok: @thejoymagnet

Facebook: @ShariAlyse

"Intuition is the bridge between what we know and what we dare to imagine."

~ **Deb DeCelle**

INTRODUCTION

Welcome to *The Intuitive Entrepreneur: Deeper Connections for Soul-Driven Success,* a book born from the shared wisdom, experiences, and breakthroughs of myself and 21 remarkable co-authors. This is more than a collection of stories; it's an invitation to step into your intuition, embrace your unique gifts, and create a soul-aligned life and business.

For many, entrepreneurship can feel overwhelming, full of challenges and uncertainty. But when intuition becomes part of the equation, those challenges transform into opportunities, and uncertainty shifts into possibility. Intuition is the quiet whisper of your soul, guiding you toward alignment, purpose, and magic. In this book, we'll explore how trusting that whisper can lead to a business and life that feels authentic, joyful, and deeply meaningful.

The Power of Yes

Each journey in this book begins with a powerful "yes"—a commitment to step forward, even when fear looms large. For me, that "yes" came during a pivotal moment in October 2022. My life then was a stark contrast to the one I live now. Working in public education felt like a daily grind, with little room for joy or purpose. My part-time work as a medium and mentor was a quiet dream, waiting for me to give it the attention it deserved. Saying "yes" to myself—to a bigger, more aligned version of my life—required courage, trust, and a willingness to embrace fear as a necessary step rather than a stopping point.

This moment, and many others like it, taught me that when you take a leap of faith, the universe rises to meet you in ways you never imagined. In my case, that leap led to launching courses, co-authoring books, mentoring clients worldwide, and even teaching at renowned spiritual centers. These opportunities didn't just show up; they were a direct result of saying "yes" and trusting my intuition to guide the way.

Your Intuition as Your Business Partner

Intuition is your greatest ally in entrepreneurship. It bridges the gap between logic and possibility, helping you navigate decisions clearly and confidently. Unlike strategy alone, which often relies on external factors, intuition taps into a more profound wisdom that aligns with your purpose and values. It's not just about making the "right" choices; it's about making the aligned choices.

In Chapter 1, "The Power of Yes: Embracing Fear as a Step, Not a Stop," I share my own transformational journey of trusting intuition over fear. You'll read about pivotal moments, like saying yes to working with a business coach when the cost seemed out of reach or opening my first office space despite lingering doubts. These experiences remind us that courage often walks hand-in-hand with fear, but we create breakthroughs in choosing courage.

The Voices of 21 Co-authors

Throughout this book, you'll meet 21 co-authors, each with their own unique story of navigating the entrepreneurial journey through the lens of intuition. From overcoming fear of failure to trusting their inner voice in the face of doubt, their stories will inspire and empower you to see your own intuition as a powerful tool for success.

You'll find practical tools, insights, and exercises designed to help you deepen your connection with your inner guidance. From techniques like virtual vision boarding to cultivating mindfulness and clarity, these chapters will equip you with actionable steps to integrate intuition into your business and daily life.

An Invitation to You

This book is an invitation to take your own leap of faith. Wherever you are on your journey, know that your intuition is already within you, waiting to guide you toward a life and business aligned with your soul's calling. As you read these stories, I encourage you to reflect on your own moments of saying yes. What opportunities are waiting for you on the other side of fear? What dreams are ready to take flight if you trust your inner compass?

Embrace the Adventure

If there's one message I hope you take from this book, it's this: Embrace the adventure. Your intuition will lead you to places you never thought possible, but only if you trust it. Say yes to yourself, to your dreams, and to the life you're meant to live. The journey may not always be easy, but I promise it will be worth it.

On behalf of myself and the 21 incredible coauthors, thank you for joining us on this journey. Together, let's explore the power of intuition and unlock the deeper connections that lead to soul-driven success.

"Courage is more exhilarating than fear, and in the long run, it is easier."

~ Eleanor Roosevelt

CHAPTER 1

THE POWER OF YES

Embracing Fear as a Step, Not a Stop

By Deb DeCelle, Educational Medium and Mentor

MY STORY

I talk to dead people every day as part of my job—a reality so surreal I sometimes must pinch myself. Just a few years ago, my life looked vastly different. Buried in the grind of public education, my role as a medium and mentor was merely a part-time gig, a quiet dream waiting in the wings. Each morning, I awoke to face an exhausting cycle of defiant students and bureaucratic red tape, a joyless routine that seemed to suck the life from me.

I can vividly recall when my part-time dream became my full-time reality. It wasn't a gradual shift but a bold leap of faith that catapulted me into a life I only dared to imagine. October 2022 became a pivotal month that altered the course of my life forever.

It began with a conversation over lunch with my dear friend Bryan, whom I deeply admired. He leaned in, his eyes lit with enthusiasm.

"Deb, if you're serious about taking things to the next level, you must meet my business coach. She's incredible—she's helped me transform my business completely. Just schedule a consultation call with her. Trust me, it'll be worth it," he said, his tone carrying the conviction of someone whose life had been profoundly changed.

Skeptical but intrigued, I nodded. "Do you think she can help me?" I asked.

"Absolutely," Bryan said firmly. "You're ready for this."

His words lingered in my mind as I scheduled the call. The next night, I sat on my couch, nervously gripping my water bottle as I waited for her to join the video call. When her face appeared on the screen, her energy was magnetic—warm, confident, and immediately inspiring.

For an hour, we dove into a vision of what could be. "Imagine this—scaling your mediumship work far beyond anything you've done before. Online courses, mentoring, teaching in incredible places, what do you think?" she asked.

"That sounds. . .incredible. But reaching a broader audience like that? It feels impossibly big," I said.

"Big, yes. Impossible? No. You're already doing the work, Deb. It's about showing up bigger and claiming your space. People need what you offer."

"It's exciting but also terrifying. What if I'm not enough for something this big?" I asked.

"You are enough. You've already built the foundation. Think about the lives you've touched, the people who've come to you for guidance. Now, imagine multiplying that."

As the call neared its end, I knew the question of cost was coming. I braced myself.

"To work with me," she said, her voice steady and confident, "my six-month fee is $4,000."

I froze, the number echoing in my mind. My pulse quickened, and I gripped the edge of the tray table in front of me. That figure was astronomical to someone like me.

I swallowed hard, trying to steady my voice. "That's. . .definitely an investment," I managed, forcing a nervous laugh.

She smiled gently. "It is. But consider this: what's the cost of staying exactly where you are? If you're ready to step into your power, this is the time to invest in yourself."

Her words hung heavy in the air long after the call ended. I paced the room, wrestling with fear and doubt. That night, I talked it over with my husband, Heath, who listened patiently before taking my hands in his.

"Deb," he said, his voice calm and steady, "you've been waiting for this moment. Your intuition is screaming at you to go for it, and I think you should; we'll figure out the money."

He was right; while talking to her, I felt waves of chills in my body, which is always my sign that I'm on the right track. That feeling for me is like when you listen to a song, and it gives you goosebumps; that is my signal.

His unwavering support and my signal from Spirit gave me the nudge I needed. Deep down, I knew the money would show up—I just had to leap.

The next morning, with my heart pounding and my palms sweating, I messaged her: "I'm in." I made my first payment, and I felt a seismic shift at that moment. Life as I knew it was about to transform.

"Everything you want is on the other side of fear."

~ Wayne Dyer

The universe responded swiftly and spectacularly. In the ten months that followed, I launched my first course, co-authored a book, joined an incredible collaborative group of international mediums, started my mentoring program, traveled to Maui, and—most importantly—left my job in public education behind.

It was as if the universe had been holding its breath, waiting for me to say "yes" to myself. And when I finally did, it was like a dam breaking—everything happened simultaneously, a whirlwind of opportunities and magic that left me in awe.

When you step fully into your passion and purpose, the universe doesn't just meet you halfway—it opens doors you didn't even know existed. Saying "yes" to ME was the single most transformative decision I've ever made, and it is proof that when you trust in the process, the results are nothing short of extraordinary.

While Heath and I were in Maui that July, a single Facebook post caught my attention and set a new course for my future. For months, I'd dreamed of finding my own "brick-and-mortar" space to meet with clients. Just the day before, Heath and I talked about it over breakfast.

"Babe, do you think I should rent a room or go all in on an office?" I asked him.

He sipped his coffee thoughtfully before replying, "Maybe start by renting a room until you leave your job and focus on mediumship full time."

Deep down, I was itching to make the leap. Scrolling through Facebook, I saw that a local grief counselor I deeply respected was looking for someone to share her office suite—there was an opening starting on September 1st.

My heart raced as I turned to Heath.

"No way," I exclaimed, holding up my phone. "You're not going to believe this! Kelly has an office available in her suite!"

His eyebrows shot up. "Really? How much is it?"

"I don't know yet," I said, unable to contain my excitement. "But I'm going to find out."

Without hesitation, I wrote an email to Kelly expressing my interest. Then came the waiting—a mix of nervous anticipation and excitement for what this opportunity could mean.

Little did I know, this was the first step toward creating a space to become the heart of my growing business.

Kelly got back to me quickly with the details, and while the price was still a bit intimidating, it felt manageable—doable. I took a deep breath and once again said, "Yes."

When Heath and I returned to the mainland, I knew I needed to discuss this with someone who had always been one of my biggest supporters—a dear friend who felt like a second father to me. Rich had been there for me through thick and thin, always cheering me on and believing in my potential, even when I doubted myself.

As I shared the opportunity with him, his eyes lit up with the same unwavering confidence I'd seen so many times before. "Are you going to do this full-time now?" he asked eagerly. "Please tell me you're finally taking the plunge."

I hesitated, wringing my hands as I replied, "I'm not sure. I don't know if I can swing it just yet."

That's when he leaned back, gave me a knowing smile, and reminded me of a promise he had made years ago. "Deb, do you remember what I told you? If you ever decide to strike out on your own, I'll help you. You were born to do this."

His words hit me like a wave, both comforting and overwhelming. I had tucked that promise away in my mind, not daring to hope it was real. But here he was, bringing it back to life.

Over the course of our conversation, he leaned forward, his voice steady and serious. "How much do you need to make this happen? Figure out a number—make sure it includes six months' rent—and consider it a zero-interest loan."

I was completely floored. My breath caught, and my chest tightened with gratitude and disbelief. He meant it. This wasn't just an offer made in passing years ago-it was real, tangible, and life-changing.

That night, I sat down with Heath and crunched the numbers, calculating what it would take to make my dream a reality. Nervously, I called my friend the next day; he chuckled warmly at my calculations and said, "Now, when can I drop off the check?"

Tears welled up in my eyes. I was utterly overwhelmed by his generosity, his belief in me, and the profound realization that someone was willing to invest in my dream so wholeheartedly. This was more than just financial help—it was the final nudge I needed to step fully into my purpose.

On August 1st, with excitement and trepidation, I drafted my resignation letter. My heart ached, knowing that after nearly 15 years, I would not return to school that September. It felt like closing the door on one chapter of my life while standing at the threshold of an entirely new one.

From that moment, life seemed to accelerate, as if the universe was eager to show me what was possible when I fully embraced my purpose. Before I knew it, I was boarding a plane to England, teaching in Costa Rica, Colorado, and at a world-renowned spiritualist center. Each experience affirmed that I was exactly where I was meant to be.

It was during the spring of the following year that I met Peggy. She arrived in my life with an openness and curiosity that I recognized immediately—a quiet knowing that she had untapped potential just waiting to be discovered. She'd been told repeatedly that she had "something there," but she didn't quite know how to access it—yet.

That's where I came in.

When Peggy signed up for three months of mentoring with me, she made a powerful choice: she said "yes" to herself. From the start, she radiated a laid-back, adventurous spirit and a heart of pure gold. Over those three special months, she deepened her belief in her abilities and allowed them to shine brighter than ever.

I'll never forget the moment she realized her true power. With tears in her eyes, she said, "I can feel it now—this has been inside me all along."

By the end of our time together, Peggy wasn't just intuitive—she was confident, empowered, and ready to embrace life in a new and intuitive way. Her transformation was a testament to what happens when someone takes that leap of faith and trusts in their own potential.

I guided Peggy to trust her inner compass and recognize that the information dropping into her mind wasn't just random nonsense shaped by her own experiences. It was real, intuitive insight. Bit by bit, she began to trust the whispers of her intuition, and the transformation was extraordinary to witness.

One day, during a practice exercise, I showed her a photo of the house where I grew up. She had no idea it was connected to me—no context, no clues. Peggy studied the image quietly before beginning to speak, describing what life was like in that house. As the words flowed, I felt a chill run down my spine. Her descriptions were eerily accurate, vividly capturing my childhood's essence.

I sat there, dumbfounded. Tears welled in my eyes as she finished.

"You nailed it," I said, my voice trembling with emotion.

She stared at me in disbelief. "Seriously? Are you kidding me?"

"No," I said, shaking my head. "Almost every single detail was spot-on."

The look on her face was priceless—a mix of shock and tentative pride as she began to grasp just how powerful her gift was.

Guiding her through an exercise to connect with my departed mother, she relayed messages and impressions using the tools I taught her. I found myself blown away once again.

When she finished, I looked at her with awe and joy. "Peggy, I can't even fathom how you didn't believe in your abilities before now. They're incredible. I guess all you needed was a little structure. You did this, Peggy. You've had the power all along."

Her eyes widened as a mix of laughter and disbelief bubbled out. "I can't believe it! When people told me I was gifted, I thought it was total BS."

My work with Peggy was about so much more than learning how to connect with departed loved ones or tap into photos intuitively. It was about helping her blend the magic of her intuition with the practicality of her everyday life.

Guiding Peggy to navigate her world with grace and resilience became a balance of two realms: 30 minutes dedicated to her everyday life and 30 minutes exploring the magic of her intuition. This split addressed her real-world stressors while nurturing her growing spiritual gifts.

During the "everyday" half, we developed mindfulness tools and strategies to help her navigate the ups and downs of daily life with compassion and clarity. Together, we unpacked the chaos of her busy world, offering her practical ways to manage her emotions, set boundaries, and reclaim her peace.

One of the most profound realizations for Peggy was understanding that she wasn't "crazy" when she felt overwhelmed by the emotions of others. As I explained the concept of being an empath, her eyes lit up with recognition.

"Wait," she said, her voice tinged with relief and curiosity, "you mean it's normal to feel like I'm carrying everyone else's emotions?"

"Yes," I said with a smile. "You're not imagining it. You've been experiencing life through a very different lens—highly sensitive and deeply intuitive—even from a young age."

It was a breakthrough moment for Peggy. She began to see her empathic nature not as a burden but as a gift she could harness and manage. Together, we worked on grounding techniques and energy-clearing practices that gave her the tools to protect her emotional well-being while embracing her natural ability to connect with others deeply.

She stepped into her power, weaving together two worlds, which was magical. She went from doubting herself completely to owning her gifts with confidence and grace. And in doing so, she didn't just transform her own life—she also opened the door to helping others in ways she never imagined.

Peggy wrote me a heartfelt letter at the end of our three transformative months together. Her words, filled with gratitude and vulnerability, remain etched in my heart as a beautiful reminder of the magic we created together.

"I want to express my sincere appreciation for you and your mentorship. I have learned so much and grown greatly over the last few months. I feel I've come in as one person and am leaving as another. Peggy"

And it was all possible because of one simple word, "yes."

THE TOOL

One of my favorite tools is virtual vision boarding. It's simple, powerful, and can transform your reality when you approach it with intention.

We spend so much time glued to these magical little rectangles we call cell phones, so why not use them to supercharge your dreams? Select your favorite digital template-based design tool; I use Canva.

1.   **Select the phone wallpaper template.**

2.   **Get crystal clear on what you want.**

3.   **Under the elements tab, search for photos that represent your desires and insert as many as you'd like.**

4.   **Hit share and download the design.**

5.   **Save it as an attachment in a draft email, then open it on your phone and save the design as your wallpaper.**

As your desires become a reality, update your virtual vision board as needed.

Here's where the real magic happens: by seeing your vision board constantly, you're keeping your goals at the forefront of your mind, aligning your energy with them, and inviting them into your reality. When you look at it, FEEL what life will be like when those visions are realized because feelings create frequency, and frequency creates your reality. Opportunities for aligned action will present themselves in the most extraordinary ways. Trust me, it works.

In the past two years, there hasn't been a single item on my virtual vision boards that hasn't manifested in my life. As soon as one dream becomes reality, I update the collage to set the next level of magic into motion.

This isn't just a tool; it's a daily ritual that reminds you of your power to create the life you want. Try it and watch your world change!

Deb DeCelle is an international educational medium and mentor.

Deb's passion is helping others unlock their intuitive potential. Her work has taken her from small-town settings in upstate New York to global stages, where she inspires clients to embrace their intuitive abilities and explore their soul's purpose. Known for her compassionate, down-to-earth approach, she offers intuitive guidance, mediumship, and personalized mentoring that empowers individuals to live authentically and fearlessly.

With dual degrees in Marketing and Management, Deb combines business expertise with profound intuitive training. She has studied extensively under the internationally renowned psychic medium Tony Stockwell and honed her abilities at two of the world's most prestigious spiritual learning centers, the Omega Institute in Rhinebeck, New York, and The Arthur Findlay College in Stansted, England.

In addition to her one-on-one work, Deb has taught internationally and at the world-renowned spiritual hub of LilyDale in Western New York. With a mission to make intuition accessible to everyone, Deb inspires others to embrace their inner gifts and live a life of deeper connection and meaning.

Connect with Deb:

Website: https://www.debdecelle.com

Facebook: https://www.facebook.com/debdecellemedium

Instagram: https://www.instagram.com/debdecellemedium

"Much madness is divinest sense to a discerning eye."

-Emily Dickinson

CHAPTER 2

WHAT SHOULD I ᴧDO?
ᴧASK YOUR ᴧBONES

Three Quick Steps to Yes (or No)

By Emily Atlantis Wolf

MY STORY

God, I'm not going to make it.

I laid my face on my white pillowcase and slid my hands under the pillow, curling my body like a flower closing its petals. The empty pillow next to me became blurry as my tears filled the cup between my eye and nose, spilling down my cheek and lips, mixing with the taste of tobacco.

I swallowed my sniffly tears, too tired to get up and walk to the bathroom and risk waking my two kids. The salty waters mixed with the last drops of gin at the back of my throat.

I need a sign. I'm at the end. At the cliff. I can't do this. No husband, no mother, no friends. There's nothing to hold on to. The kids will be okay with their dad, right?

The answer rang in my skull like a cathedral bell, resounding in shuddering waves from head to toe as if I was an acolyte crouched and hiding in the corner of a tower at midnight.

No! No, they won't!

I cried the tears of a mother who lost her mother and has no other mothers to care for her.

I'm fine. It's fine.

The day started fine. I was up at 5:15 am to get ready for the hour-long commute to work. I put on one of my two pairs of dress pants and pulled a shirt off the pile of clean clothes on top of the storage bench next to my bed. I brushed my teeth, fluffed my hair, fed my cats, and kissed my kids goodbye.

"Daddy will be here soon to get you ready for school," I said to each of them as a prayer and assertion, hugging their soft, warm bodies in bed.

I drove down the highway, looking forward to seeing the vista of the Cuyahoga Valley National Park as I drove over the interstate bridge. Miles of trees on either side of the river gave me the sensation of timelessness. It was rush, rush, rush until these moments when I could breathe one breath in peace. The quiet giants calmed my thoughts and cleared my mind as I drove through the dips and curves.

I was at my desk in the Project Services department before BJ marched by like a prison guard, coffee in one hand while the other long arm swung like a club at his side.

"Morning!" I said, looking up from my emails on the computer screen.

He nodded.

With my unofficial check-in passed, I left my beige cubicle walls and black office chair to go downstairs for breakfast. As I reached for the stairwell door, someone was pulling it open from the other side. A second before I saw a face, I heard a voice screaming in my head.

Burn the witch!

Rebecca appeared in the doorway.

"Morning," I said as she strode past me, unacknowledged.

Whoa. What the hell was that?

Feeling shaky and rattled, I got breakfast and sat back at my desk, overhearing Ruth on the other side of the cubicle wall.

"He's good, Mom, you know, busy. Still always talking about going fishing in Michigan. Maybe next year," said Ruth.

Michigan is two hours away. Who doesn't have time for a weekend trip two hours away?

My boss, JP, came smiling like Shakespeare's Puck and put his hand on my wall.

"Morning!" he said. "How are you?"

"I'm good," I said. "My birthday's next week."

"Oh, an Aquarius! My mom's an Aquarius. She's 94. I should call her."

She's 94? Call her every day!

"Hey, can you stand in for Mary at the monthly status meeting today?" he said. "She's out."

"Yep, no problem," I said.

"It's in the big conference room. Only 250 people in the seats and 5,000 people on the call."

"No problem."

I would follow that man into a holy war.

I sat next to Rebecca for the status meeting.

"Hey, Rebecca, is JP going to be at the walkthrough this afternoon?" I asked.

She was reading the meeting agenda and didn't look up.

"No, BJ is leading. DW is the SME for programmers, CJ is the SME for architecture, and DEO is subbing for DBO as sponsor."

She looked at me sideways.

"Are you sure you can handle it? Mary's out today."

"I heard. Yep, no problem. Any execs at the meeting?"

"Lisa Dallas and Jim McCool."

VP of Retirement Services and CFO. Okay. Good to know.

When it was my turn to get up and speak, I walked to the podium and adjusted the mic.

"Hello everyone. I'm standing in for Mary Crawford today to talk about…"

"Yes, latte, no foam, extra hot," said a faceless man's voice, interrupting the call into the conference room.

"As a gentle reminder," I said, "Please mute your phone after you call in by pressing star 69."

I paused.

"The Sponsor Fee Disclosure project is on target for tiered deployment, starting…"

"No, I need the papers now!" said a woman's voice on the call.

"That's star 69," I said slowly. "Starting in mid-March, two test environments…"

"That's not what I said!" said another man with construction sounds behind him.

"Or, just hang up the phone," I said as a giggle of laughter rippled through the room.

After the meeting, a man in a suit with a practiced smile approached me. "You sure handled that well. And no notes! I haven't seen you before. Who are you?"

"I wrote the project requirements document. I'm a BA in Project Services. I work for JP."

"Okay," he said, still smiling. "Well, I'm going to keep my eye on you."

"Well, I'm a contractor. Schwab doesn't hire contractors. Not here, at least."

"We could change that," he said, extending his hand. "I'm Jim McCool."

I shook his hand, looking into his eyes with the beginning of a smile.

Don't yank my chain, Zeus.

After a seamless afternoon walkthrough meeting and a final check of emails, I was ready to leave.

I drove home, scanning the valley of trees again, the sea of green verdure rolling into the river. A hawk glided across the sky, tilting his wings. His white feathered belly caught the long, golden rays of the setting sun.

I want to know how that feels.

As I made my way back to the city, the divided highway turned into a four-lane boulevard that turned into a street with sidewalks and century trees.

I love my neighborhood. It always feels like a nest.

I drove into the parking lot of Fernway Elementary School to pick up my kids from aftercare in the gym.

5:57! I'm not late.

As I opened the door and raised a hand in greeting to the three proctors, I saw my son, Paul, playing four square with two other kids, a girl and a boy. Paul turned his moon-shaped face to me, and I lit up like the sun.

"Mama!" he said, turning to run to me.

At that moment, I saw the boy watching Paul. He slammed the ball onto the floor, causing it to bounce up and hit my son in the face.

In two quick steps, I was bent down, holding all of Paul, who was thunderstruck. Sophia, my daughter, cut over and said, "Hi Mama! What happened?"

I looked at the boy, bigger than Paul. In a sound closer to a growl than a voice, I said, "Why did you do that?"

He said nothing intelligible.

"Get over there and sit down," I said, pointing to the long cafeteria-style table.

This shit of a mongrel!

He walked to the end and sat at the small round seat attached to the table. I sat across from him with my right arm around Paul's waist, who was standing next to me. Sophia was standing on my left.

"Do you know who this is?" I said to the boy, pointing at Paul.

"No," he said with his hands in his lap.

"This is Paul. And I am his mother. You don't hurt him, you don't upset him, you don't make fun of him, you don't make him uncomfortable, and you don't bother him. Ever. Do you understand? Ever. Am I clear?"

"Mmm-mm," said the boy still looking at me.

"Now say you're sorry."

"I'm sorry," he said to me.

"Not to me!" I said, pointing to Paul. "To him!"

"I'm sorry," he said before looking back at me.

"It's okay," said Paul with his characteristic 10,000-watt moonbeam smile.

I pointed to my kindergartener Sophia, who was rocking happily up on her toes and back on her heels, unflustered. "And this is my daughter, Sophia. All the same policies apply."

As I stood up to leave, the door to the gym opened, and a woman in dress pants, a top, and a long elegant coat appeared. I watched as her son stood up and ran over, pointing to me.

Without taking my eyes off her, I said to my kids, "Pick up your backpacks and get in the car. It's unlocked."

They both walked with quick steps to the door, grabbed their backpacks from the bench, and left. I stood there watching this woman like an alpha wolf standing on a ridge.

Fuck with me, Lady. I dare you.

She looked at her son, listening. She looked at me, then steered him toward the door, scooping up his backpack on the way out.

Hope that little fucker's father isn't a lawyer. Did I say anything illegal? Agh.

With hot blood and a cool demeanor, I drove us two blocks home. The kids ran into the house to throw off their coats and find the cats. I brought in the bags, took off my shoes, and hung up my coat.

"Who wants chicken and mac and cheese?" I hollered up the stairs to

their bedrooms.

"Me!" said Paul.

"Me, me, me!" said Sophia.

After changing clothes, I cooked up the organic chicken as water boiled for the pasta in the box of organic mac and cheese. We ate dinner in the dining room, and I listened to the kid's stories, nourished by their presence.

You are the stars in my dark sky.

They played in the house while I washed dishes and cleaned the kitchen. At 7:30 pm, I said, "Bedtime! Get ready for bed then you can pick out a book to read."

I went to Paul's room and sat on his bed. We read Mañana Iguana, by Ann Whitford Paul. He laughed as always at the comical expressions of frustration on the main character, a female iguana trying to get help as she puts together a party for her town. I kissed his soft, round face and hugged his whole body in my arms, feeling happy to be with him.

"Love you, Mama!"

"Love you, too, Angel."

I went to Sophia's room and sat on her bed. We read Mama, Do You Love Me? By Barbara Joosse. She pointed out wolves, puffins, and bears related to the Inuit story of a daughter who wants to hear how many ways her mother loves her. I kissed her delicate doll face, which looked more like my mother than me. She traced my face with her finger, making up a song with only the sounds "dee-dah-dum-deedy-de-da" until landing on my nose, giggling.

"Love you, Mama!" she said as she tossed her naked body on its side and covered herself with her security blanket. I tucked her in, marveling at her beauty.

"Love you, too, Baby."

I walked downstairs into the clean kitchen and grasped a bottle of Tanqueray gin from the cabinet over the fridge. I poured it into a juice glass over ice with club soda and a squeeze of lime. Walking out the back door and into the garage behind the house, I brought down a planter full of twigs and sticks for making fires. In it was a box of American Spirit cigarettes with a lighter.

With my drink and box of cigarettes, I walked two steps outside the garage and climbed up on the hood of the white, 25-year-old, lowered-chassis Acura Integra left by my ex-husband.

I hate this car.

With my back on the windshield, I looked into the night sky and sighed a long sound as if I had been holding my breath since I woke up.

I'm not going to make it.

I put on headphones and listened to "Mad World," the Donnie Darko movie theme, while I smoked, had my drink, and looked into the heavens. "... the dreams in which I'm dying are the best I ever had." I lit a second cigarette and listened to "Somewhere Over Rainbow," sung by Israel Kamakawiwo'ole. "... Birds fly over the rainbow, why then, oh why, can't I?"

Somewhere is a place where I get through this. Where I'm okay. Where I'm divorced, doing something I love, walking the kids to school, no aftercare. Maybe happy. I feel it. I'm going to make it. I don't know how to get there. Or what it looks like. God, I'm tired.

I put everything away and went to bed. The tears—missing for a year since my mom's funeral—came through me like a river. Without a reason, my protective barriers collapsed under a wave of emotions that I held at bay so I could keep going to work and keep picking up my kids.

God, tell me what to do, and I'll do it. I need to stay in this house with my kids and make enough money to survive. I'm done. I can't figure this out alone. I'll do anything you want.

I cried into unconsciousness.

I awoke before my alarm in a room full of white light, as if I was at the center of a pulsing dandelion, a sparkling ball filled with thin, luminous energies. I sat up on my elbow and looked around. On my pillow were two words written in thick white cursive letters with silver edging: Massage Therapist.

I knew this was the answer. My body felt electrified and light. A sense of knowing filled my bones. I went to work and gave Lisa Dallas one day's notice with apologies because I found a medical massage program that started in three days. I never looked back.

THE TOOL

When I access my intuition, my answer comes as a deep knowing in my bones. I feel the answer. Then comes the seeing from my third eye with my two eyeballs open or closed. I see spiritual beings, power animals, dragons, and angels and telepathically receive messages from them. I can see past and future versions of clients and their ancestors. My gifts are a result of natural ability, curiosity, and practice. With a few simple steps, you can begin your journey of connecting your physical experiences to non-physical realities.

As a Seneca Wolf Clan ordained Shamanic Minister, I call upon Grandmother Spider:

Grandmother Spider, weaver of the cosmic web of life connecting all beings as one family, we call to you with love and gratitude. Guide our journey to knowing. Teach us the magic of web-making, weaving, and waiting for the miraculous answers to arrive. Help us create a strong connection between our past and future ancestors so we may honor this fleeting, precious time with Mother Earth. Illuminate our playful and curious nature to discover creative solutions. O Mitake Oyasun.

Think of a question. If you are new at harnessing your intuition, ask a question that can be answered with yes or no.

Step 1: Get Quiet

Place both hands on your chest and close your eyes. Bring your love and attention to this general part of your body. Breathe normally, allowing your inhales and exhales to slow to a comfortable rhythm. Focus on feeling the heartbeats, the ribs rising and falling, and the touch of your hand on your skin.

Keep breathing and feeling until you feel more sensations. Notice if your hands are getting warmer or your torso feels bigger. Get curious about what else you can sense. Keep your focus centered inside your body. If there are sounds or distractions outside your body, practice letting them be there while staying focused on your breathing lungs and beating heart.

Step 2: Get Still

After you feel centered and quiet, put both hands on your belly. Close your eyes. Breathe in. As you exhale, make the 'om' sound. Make a game out of breathing out as long and slow as you can, pausing at the end to feel your body.

After your belly feels still, place your hands back on your chest. Breathe in. Breathe out making the 'ah' sound. Play the game again, exhaling longer and louder. Pause after the loudest 'ah' sound and feel your body.

After your heart feels still, place the first two fingers from each hand at the beginning of each eyebrow, close to the top of your nose. Close your eyes. Placing love and attention on your forehead, make the 'ee' sound. Again, long and slow exhales as you make the sound. Pause and feel your mind. When your mind feels still, move to step 3.

Step 3: Get Clear

Placing your hands on your chest again, close your eyes. Ask your heart your question. Wait for a reply. Use this format, "My wise and intuitive Heart, detached from the outcome, answer my question: [State your question.]"

Sense the answer with your whole body.

You may get a vision, a word, or a sensation of warm or cool tingles on your skin. Stay open and curious about how the answer arrives. Be patient and alert. Journal your experience to discover more information. If no message comes through, repeat the steps when you are well-rested.

I'm Atlantis Wolf, and I believe in you.

Emily Atlantis Wolf is an intuition teacher and retreat leader. Her education spans a BS in Civil Engineering from Pennsylvania State University to a medical massage therapist license from the State Medical Board of Ohio. Her certifications include Master Breathwork Facilitator and Ordained Shamanic Minister from Linda Star Wolf at Venus Rising, Usui Reiki Master trained by William Lee Rand, and Emotion Code Practitioner trained by Dr. Bradley Nelson.

She has been in private practice since 2010 and has helped over 3500 people with chronic or acute pain issues. Her work has shifted over the years from one-to-one sessions to group work, including writing courses, breathwork and cacao events, and global retreats.

Atlantis created Intuition Academy, a year-long program for clients to discover and hone their innate intuitive abilities so they can meet their personal goals, make executive decisions with confidence, and repair ancestral wounds. Students move from basic skills (Big Yes and Big No), to intermediate (What About Maybe?) to advanced skills (Angels, Dragons, and Spirit Guides). Students have the option to repeat the program to master the skills at every level.

Connect with Emily Atlantis:

To learn more about Intuition Academy: www.atlantiswolf.com

To learn about retreats, breathwork events, and fire ceremonies: www.atlantiswolf.com

To book a discovery call: https://sanototum.fullslate.com/employees/2

"Be an encourager, the world has plenty of critics already."

~ Dave Willis

CHAPTER 3

TEAM SPIRIT

Becoming an Epic Collaborator

By Julie Speetjens, Creator of Soul Journey Sundays

Hi, my name is Julie Speetjens, and I'm a recovering people-pleaser and perfectionist. The Universe literally put me in a wheelchair to get me to slow down, tune in, and step out of my destructive loop of self-doubt, external validation, and frenetic effort.

I wasn't "born" a psychic medium; rather, my intuitive abilities spontaneously blossomed in my early forties, soon after my Reiki Master training. Anyone can learn how to tune into their intuition and powerful tools are available for you. I hope the following pages will help you discover your soul purpose, strength, and tribe—that you will give yourself permission to turn down the volume on your inner critic and foster collaboration instead of competition. It's my heartfelt desire that you'll be inspired to take one joyful dance step closer to your divine soul-self and bask in the magic you've been seeking.

MY STORY

I love being a cheerleader, and not the sparkly pom-poms and jaw-dropping gymnastics type. I mean, it fundamentally makes my soul happy to uplift and empower people, to help ignite the divine spark within them and watch them soar. I suppose I'm trying to be the woman I needed as a child.

In my quest for understanding, I've encountered many modalities that each offered some measure of insight. Ask Human Design and I'm a Manifesting Generator; astrology will tell you that I'm a Virgo with Scorpio rising; Myers-Briggs indicates that I'm an INFJ-A, and the Enneagram says I'm a Type 3.

Ask a psychologist and sometimes it seems like my personality is just a big pile of trauma responses—hyper-independent with an avoidant attachment style. Dr. Gary Chapman would tell you my love languages are gifts and acts of service. I've spent decades interpreting myself, the people around me, and the meaning of life.

My major in college was environmental science, and I wanted to save the world one recycled can at a time. Having become a Reiki Master teacher, psychic medium, and spiritual event coordinator, I realize I'm still trying to save the world—just one chakra and one reading at a time instead.

Throughout my life, I've pushed myself to the brink of exhaustion in a misguided attempt to prove my worth and earn love and approval. Scholastically, personally, and professionally, I've been a slave to productivity and a relentless drive to be the best. My husband used to call me "General Julie," and it was not a term of endearment.

Long story short, my inner critic was a chatty bitch:

I need straight A's.
I should be thinner.
I shouldn't have said that.
It's my fault.
I'm not smart enough.
They don't like me.
I can't sing.
My house should be cleaner.
I'm hard to love.
I have to earn more money.
Who am I to do that?
I'm not special.

Sound familiar? Do you relentlessly torture yourself with negative thoughts and emotions like I did?

As I learned to walk again after consecutive hip surgeries and found Reiki (or it found me), my healing journey skyrocketed, and my mediumship abilities suddenly opened. My shift from corporate to cosmic began with a bang!

As a former IT Project Manager who spent years commuting from Colorado to Manhattan, I threw myself into every psychic and mediumship class, practice circle, and mentorship I found. I had finally discovered the key to my spiritual gifts and the missing piece of the happiness puzzle! *It's passion, not obsession,*

I reassured myself.

Why was I so fascinated? Because it wasn't about *me*. Being a Reiki healer and a psychic medium means learning to become a channel in service of Spirit. It's about setting aside your thinking mind, expectations, assumptions, limiting beliefs, and fears. I always tell my students, "Get out of your head and into your heart." As well-educated as you may be, in the role of intuitive healer, no one cares what you think. They care what you can perceive in the energy, what you can discern from a higher perspective, and what you can allow to flow through you for their highest good. There can be no judgment. For an over-thinker like me, it's bliss.

Being in the zone, the power, or the flow state while giving Reiki or a reading is like smoothly snowboarding down a beautiful mountain with perfect powder on a crisp, bluebird day. It's an explosive breath of fresh air after being held underwater too long. It's the relief of a cool drink on a parched throat in the blistering heat of August. It's a sacred liminal space where relentless self-criticism and self-doubt are paused, and unconditional love swells within. It's a precious moment of expansive freedom that propels me out of the mundane, beyond superficial interaction and physical limitations—when I stop resisting joy and embrace divinity. It's the home I yearned for and the magic that was missing.

Receiving a great reading can save people decades of anguish. It can lift the odious weight of grief they've carried through Hell. Energy healing and intuitive artistry are doorways to wonder. Unleashing the imagination, giving people reason to hope, seek, and allow. It breathes life back into the lifeless, light into the darkness, color into grayness, emotion into numbness, connection into loneliness, love into apathy, and hope into despair. Everyone needs to experience it to believe it; they have to feel it to dare to receive it.

There is simply no better feeling! I want to shout it from the rooftops. So, just 18 months after my first spontaneous mediumistic experience, my Spirit Team nudged me to start an online psychic mediumship event called "Soul Journey Sundays" (SJS).

As a side note, we all have an amazing Spirit Team of soul friends, angels, helpers, and teachers. Learning to trust their subtle nudges, signs, and inspirations is a fun and worthwhile endeavor that can powerfully guide your life and your business. I have lots of stories of these God-winks and wow moments, but they're for another book.

SJS started with a small group of my incredible colleagues. One of whom I was recently discussing it with said, "Can you believe we started with just a handful of us in mainland USA, and we've grown to over 60 Readers from all over the world? We're in Hawaii, Canada, England, Ireland, Turkey, and

Sweden, it's awesome!" SJS has reached over 1,000 event participants, many of whom have been profoundly affected by the healing, insights, and divine validations received in readings. It has truly been a labor of love, and I'm just glad to be part of it.

For the public, the SJS events and website have become a vibrant platform where they can easily and confidently reach a wide variety of highly trained, vetted, and experienced Intuitive Artists. For the SJS Team, it has created a community where we can brainstorm, share resources, explore ideas and experiences, encourage each other, and refer clients. In a recent conversation with a fellow SJS Reader, she said, "Just think of all the fun and amazing opportunities we would have missed if you hadn't followed the nudge and started SJS!" It has become an incubator that honors collaboration over competition and promotes bravery and growth.

If I have a client seeking a skill beyond my sphere, I poll the SJS Team and find it. When I have a co-teaching opportunity and want to assemble a diverse and fabulous group, I know where to go. When a publisher or podcaster is looking for valuable contributions, guess where my compass needle points? A New York Times journalist recently interviewed me and asked if I knew any other great folks to speak with, and I said, "Man, do I?! Only about 60!" We're helping propel each other beyond our imaginations.

When I shifted out of the competitive corporate world, it would've been easy to bring that mindset with me into my new practice: to maintain the ideal of "snake or be snaked," to assume that someone's gain was my loss, to work within the framework that resources are limited and I should protect my piece of the pie at all costs. But I chose to drop that like a hot rock.

Part of the wisdom I found through Reiki is that this is actually an abundant Universe, that we're powerful co-creators in our own experience, and that the world needs all the healers and all the healing it can get. As a dear friend, fellow SJS reader, and lead author on this very book recently reminded me, "Collaboration will take you places that competition never will."

With SJS, I get to be a cheerleader on a whole new level. Because I'm not just promoting my wonderfully talented colleagues, I'm promoting Spirit. It's a platform to shine a spotlight on the infinite potential available within each of us, to share the truth that we are all divine, eternal soul beings. Death is not the end, and you are not alone.

SJS is more than just an event to me. I am co-creating my high-vibe tribe—a heart-centered and soul-abundant group of healers devoted to serving something bigger than themselves. I'm determined to maintain a safe space to uplift each other and be authentic, where integrity is expected, and uniqueness is celebrated. As I recently encouraged an SJS Reader/friend to be bold and step into her passion as a speaker and teacher, she said, "I'm so inspired and grateful that you won't let me hide; you gently nudge me to be me."

In the world of spiritual entrepreneurship, having a support system like this is vital because there is still ignorance and suspicion around the work we do. Coming out of the spiritual closet can be daunting, and not everyone in your sphere will be willing to adjust the version of you that they've constructed in their minds. A few years ago, I was at dinner with a former corporate colleague from my NYC days. As we perused the menus, considering our options, I blurted out that I was a Psychic Medium. He stared at me blankly, as if his mind had skipped a beat. Utterly unprepared for that shocking revelation, and at a loss to respond intelligently, he simply said, "I think I'll have the steak." Some people just aren't ready for it, and that's okay—maybe in their next life.

Surprisingly, and deeply disappointingly, you may even encounter competitiveness and territorialism among other spiritual practitioners. Not everyone will cheer you on, and some people may even resent your efforts to think bigger. You may interact with folks who are threatened by your non-competitiveness. It always stuns me, as you'd think anyone devoting themselves to service would have healed the aspects of self that need to feel superior. Not everyone is walking the talk. I choose to show up in my life the same way I taught my kids, "Lift each other up, don't tear each other down." We're all always students; be teachable.

Your light may irritate some peoples' demons; keep shining anyway.

When I started my first studio space, offering Reiki healing and psychic medium readings within the existing Lotus Center for Well-Being, the aesthetician and masseuse lost clients who felt a witch had been hired. Trolls on the internet will say incredibly harsh things that cut to the core if you allow it. Luckily, someone's inability to see your worth does not diminish your value. While my family and friends are thankfully supportive and curious about the work I do, they still occasionally say insensitive things out of ignorance rather than malice. When these things happen, I hold this powerful motto in my mind: this work requires having the heart of a butterfly and the skin of a rhino.

Growing up in a military family and always being the new kid at school, with a home life that was largely built on a foundation of criticism, passive-aggression, and sarcasm, and then working in the male-dominated corporate world, I've constructed layers of unhealthy coping mechanisms and defenses to protect myself. However, working in the intuitive realms requires that you tear down those walls and willingly open yourself to work from an expansive and unconditionally loving heart space. It simultaneously both challenges and empowers you to heal yourself mentally, physically, emotionally, and energetically. It doesn't just invite; it demands that you step out of your comfort zone, get out of your limited human mind and wounded ego, and connect soul-to-soul with your clients.

How did I overcome my fear, guardedness, lack-mentality, self-doubt, and relentlessly critical inner mean girl?

THE TOOL

Honestly, Reiki is my home base. It has been the springboard to my spiritual awakening, and I simply can't overstate what a powerful tool it is for you to explore on your healing journey. It's why I teach it and why I will forever be grateful for it. However, the education and attunements required to tap into its potential are beyond the scope of this chapter. So, I will offer you another gift instead. One that you can do in your mind, anywhere, anytime, and it will change your life.

You've heard of the Law of Attraction, right? Well, it actually works. Employing the science of deliberate intention and the art of allowing has inspired my shift from limited to limitless. I've become a devotee of Esther/Abraham Hicks, Sara Landon, and Louise Hay because I've seen the power of positive affirmation work in my life and in the lives of my clients and students, time and time again. It has helped me see how gorgeous, generous, easy, playful, and wonderful life can be. In short, I want to help you fall in love with your life again. I want you to flirt with the Universe.

Taking Your Power Back from Your Thought-Emotion Loops

Taking my power back from my thought-emotion loops was essential to my healing. Most people are unaware of what they're thinking most of the time, and their inner voice tends to be diminishing. You are not the voice inside your head. It is largely comprised of other people's fears, expectations, and limiting beliefs that you have incorporated into your story. You don't have to believe everything you think.

You have likely practiced some of these negative storylines so many times that you believe them to be true. They might not be, and regardless, they don't serve you. Once, in meditation, I visualized putting duct tape over my inner critic's mouth. I had simply heard enough. She'd had 40+ years of dominating my mind, and I was sick of her. She was a lousy roommate.

By taking a step back and witnessing your fearful patterns, and intentionally flipping the script to make your head a kinder place to be, you'll be amazed at the joy and success you usher into your experience. Emotions are a choice, and your thoughts nourish them. Worrying is not preparing you for the worst, it's worshipping the problem and magnetizing it to you.

When you catch yourself stepping into a destructive thought-emotion loop, you can pause, flip the script, and replace it with a better-feeling thought. You get back what you put out, so even if you have to fake it 'til you make it, becoming intentional with your mental and emotional landscape is essential.

This practice doesn't mean you will never have destructive thoughts again, but it does empower you to recognize, embrace, release, and transcend them. It's not toxic positivity; it's mental and emotional accountability.

So, grab your sparkly pom-poms and try these on for size:

I am enough.
I am worthy.
I am perfectly imperfect.
I am loved, loving, and lovable.
I am safe, I am happy, I am healthy, I am holy.
I am eager to see how the Universe will surprise and delight me today.
I am a powerful healer/psychic/medium/...................(fill in the blank).
My heart is overflowing with gratitude, wonder, and excitement.
Everything is always working out for me.
I deserve to be healthy and wealthy.
I deserve all the blessings the Universe has to offer me.
Spirit is excited to work with me, and evidence flows easily through me.
I am a divine, eternal soul-being, and all my life experiences serve my soul's growth and evolution.
I am calm, confident, compassionate, and clearly connected.
Fabulous opportunities and inspirations are headed my way.
I'm grateful for where I am, and excited about where I'm going.
I am open to collaboration, and fabulous people want to work with me.
My Spirit Team is amazing and works miracles for me.
My love will be graciously received.
I trust myself, my Team, and Spirit.
I choose love over fear.
I am love, I am light.
All is well.

How does that feel? Ready to do a backflip? Now, make it your own and go heal the world!

After several non-starter attempts at therapy and devouring a small library of self-help books, it has been my deep dive into spirituality and metaphysics that has crafted a lens of grace and a broader vision of the roles we all play. Rather than being mired in resentment, nursing the treasured wounds of my youth, I found freedom through forgiveness and then realized there was nothing to forgive. It has all served me. It all steered me to become the brave healer that I am today, and she's my favorite version of myself so far. I wish the same for you.

Julie Speetjens, KRMT, CMRM, LRM, ARP, is the creator and host of Soul Journey Sundays. She is a Karuna Reiki Master Teacher, Certified Medical Reiki Master, and the U.S. PR Assistant to Tony Stockwell. She has studied the Intuitive Arts at the internationally acclaimed Arthur Findlay College in England and the Omega Institute in New York. She is honored to have taught Reiki and psychic mediumship development not only at the iconic Lily Dale Assembly in New York but also internationally. She has co-created spiritual retreats and workshops in Colorado, Arizona, New Mexico, Maryland, Hawai'i, Costa Rica, Mexico, and Japan. Julie has also served as the Program Director for LifeSpark Cancer Resources. In her free time, she has provided Reiki as a volunteer at UC Health Memorial Hospital Central in the Outpatient Infusion Center as well as for participants of the LifeSpark Cancer Resources program.

Connect with Julie and/or attend a Soul Journey Sundays event:

Websites: https://www.SoaringHeartEnergies.com
https://www.SoulJourneySundays.com

Facebook: https://www.facebook.com/SoaringHeartEnergies
https://www.facebook.com/groups/594432038443222

Instagram: https://www.instagram.com/SoaringHeartEnergies
https://www.instagram.com/SoulJourneySundays

CHAPTER 4

TURN CHAOS INTO CONFIDENCE

Building Heart-Centered Intuition

By Kristin Rosmorduc, M.C.P.C., Intuitive Empowerment Coach

The world is currently experiencing a transformative spiritual awakening. In these times of profound change, the need for creative solutions to help co-create is more crucial than ever. The world calls for us to tap into our creativity and collaborate to devise innovative solutions. This isn't just a call to action but a new source of inspiration and motivation for each of us. Embracing this transformative power of personal growth can inspire and motivate us to trust our intuition and embrace our unique paths in life.

MY STORY

I learned to read auras when I was nine years old. I was a sensitive child connected to spirits, animals, and nature, so reading auras didn't seem weird or complicated. My mother told me my parents didn't know how to relate to me initially.

When I was five, Mom became interested in alternative spirituality and astrology. Then, she better understood me when she learned about all this exciting new information from the people who shared it. Despite this acceptance at home, it took me years to understand, integrate, trust, and use my intuition. I felt "weird" and rejected my intuitive inclinations in favor of trying to appear "normal." It was hard to do with a mother who openly talked about her past lives with strangers and a father who spoke with a French accent.

I could always feel what others were feeling and thinking, which was often in contrast to what they were saying. I sometimes initially could tell if classmates

33

were insincere and flattering me but were jealous and turned on me or if teachers didn't like children. I would get a feeling that something wasn't right or a sense when a friend needed encouragement without mentioning it. I was earnest and trusting, so I became confused when someone said or did something I sensed wasn't in alignment with what was happening under the surface. I also felt other people's hidden talents or pieces of themselves they didn't show. When I ignored my intuition, my confusion developed into anxiety, depression, and even physical illness. The fact was, when I didn't listen to my heart, my body rebelled. It took me years to understand that I was an intuitive empath.

"To thine own self be true."

(Shakespeare, Hamlet, 1.3.84)

Dance and theater were a welcome respite from school. Dance and theater were intuitive impulses I didn't ignore, and when I was five, I begged my mom to put me in ballet class for a year. Shakespeare became my favorite playwright. "To thine own self be true" is one of my favorite quotes. Shakespeare does not advise narcissism but to follow your heart and talents and act with integrity; I couldn't agree more.

How often do we hear advice? "Don't lose your head; don't wear your heart on your sleeve." Traditional society usually prizes the left brain logic over right brain intuition. The heart is our soul's voice, which is connected to God or source, and listening to this voice is the secret to living authentic, abundant lives. What leads us astray is not our hearts but often our egos. Listening to our beautiful soul-inspired voices through our hearts takes practice. Once we connect to our souls through our hearts, we can use our intellect to put things into action.

Well-meaning parents, teachers, friends, coaches, and other societal figures can disrupt our intuitive voices. For instance, a parent might discourage a child's artistic pursuits to favor a more 'practical' career, or a teacher might dismiss a student's gut feeling about a situation in their lives. We can learn a lot from people with more experience than us. They can offer valuable guidance, but it's essential to understand the difference between what someone else wants or believes is better for us and what we genuinely wish to or think is better for ourselves. This awareness and practice of discernment can help us navigate these influences with caution and mindfulness, empowering us to make our own decisions.

Media and social media offer enormous challenges and can disrupt our intuition.

My mother was an intelligent, educated woman and a reluctant stay-at-home mom who worked part-time at a health food store. Through this job, she met a new world of psychics, channelers, astrologers, yoga teachers, healers, etc. She took astrology classes and attended spiritual meetings. Because my dad was away on business frequently, my mom took my sister and me to some of her meetings.

My father was a wonderful, loving man but strict. I describe him as a humanist wrapped in the traditional cloak of a strict French Catholic upbringing. Education and career achievement were de facto expectations. The arts, history, humanities, and different cultures were considered essential to a well-rounded education but not as a serious career path. He was a self-taught artist and an excellent writer but too busy providing for a family. He frequently said, "When I retire, I will do my art."

My mom was a talented astrologer but never earned a living from her gift. She would lament, "I would love to build my astrology practice and do my work that I feel called to do." My father supported her having a career if she wanted, but not with the choice of astrology. His traditional Catholic upbringing caused him much fear around alternative spirituality. There were many arguments in our home, with my dad yelling, "Astrology is bull; you are listening to the wrong people."

Dad had excellent instincts but would never have called them intuition. I remember him telling us that "he could sense danger" while standing guard in the French army. I would defend my mom, "Dad, you go to church and believe in God, Saints, and angels. Metaphysics is also spiritual." So, I grew up around subliminal messages about negating intuition and the necessity of following traditional career paths. Dad loved profoundly but feared anything that wasn't taught in the church and wanted to ensure my sister and I were prepared for life.

My upbringing was a balancing act, with my feet on different sides of a fence. My mother's growing openness to alternative spirituality meant she was more aware of how to support me. However, terms like "empathic" weren't part of our vocabulary, so there wasn't much guidance on why I was so sensitive and how to deal with it. I was eager to please my dad and avoid his colorful French expressions of disapproval. I tried to fit in at school, constantly teetering on a rational vs. intuitive see-saw. Honoring my intuition, which was more natural, often led to a battle of wills.

I understand my parents' struggle with societal pressures, and I want you to know that if you're on this journey, you're not alone.

"Your positive traits are the key to your destiny. They point out what nature has best equipped you to do in this life."

Dr. Leon Masters, Founder of the University of Metaphysics

We're all divinely unique, and no other person is like you. Pretty amazing! Media, sports figures, and other well-meaning people often drown out our uniqueness and heart-based voices. We frequently deny ourselves due to a need for acceptance. Finding a way to connect with our heart-soul voices takes discernment. It took trial and error (sometimes much error) to feel, trust, and use my intuition to help make decisions. In my junior year of high school, I had a choice of taking either chemistry or another science. I let my counselor talk me into chemistry even though I hated it. I nearly failed chemistry, and that dropped my grade average. Remember, it's okay to make mistakes on your journey to self-discovery. Each mistake is a stepping stone to understanding your true self.

We strengthen our connection to our intuition through support and practice. Later, I'll share a simple technique my mother taught me to connect with and trust this voice when my thoughts are chaotic. It's evolved over the years. I haven't always used it, especially when I was younger, and fitting in was important. When I did use it, it worked like a charm.

The first time I used this technique in a situation with serious financial and interpersonal consequences was during my junior year at Michigan State University (MSU). I was accepted to a few universities but chose MSU because "it's a Big 10 University." MSU wasn't U of M (where most of my family went). I went to MSU, but not with genuine, heartfelt excitement (my ego had the reins).

MSU was fun the first year because it was new, but I felt lost. The campus is vast, with 40,000 undergraduates. There were between 200-500 students in many of my classes. The professors looked like tiny robots standing in the distance of huge auditoriums. I was constantly distracted and disconnected. It was hard to engage with professors and a sea of anonymous students. I had difficulty living in large, noisy dorms where I had trouble sleeping and getting peace. I had no place to rest and connect with myself. It was not a good learning environment for me. Each fall, I dreaded returning but felt I had to.

I made it through my first year, my second year, and then into my third. I withered more and more each term I spent there. Headaches and an eating disorder plagued me.

I knew MSU wasn't my place, but I felt stuck. *"How do I quit before the end of my third year? My parents invested so much money."*

My father was very keen on me finishing. I didn't want to disappoint him, but something had to give.

My father has always had a significant influence on me. He was very loving but firm, "Ma fille (my little girl in French), one must finish one's education to get a good job with health benefits and a pension." My mother was much less focused on how things appeared to others and following traditional paths. I finally told her how I felt and that my grades were suffering.

During spring break of my third year, my father was on a business trip overseas. I had a horrible feeling that if I went back, I'd fall into quicksand and suffocate. I also longed to return to my beloved dance school close to home. My mother told me to breathe and try to erase all the chaotic thoughts from my head and then asked, "If you could do anything you wanted, what would you do?" That exercise gave my heart the freedom to express itself; I said, "I don't want to return after the break." Then, Mom asked, "How does that decision feel in your body?"When I thought about not returning to MSU, I relaxed, and my solar plexus and heart felt light—immediate relief, happiness, and freedom. Thankfully, my mom said, "That's what you will do."

Besides angering my dad, several other concerns blocked my intuition: the optics of quitting before I graduated and leaving my boyfriend. I shared a lease on an apartment that didn't expire until summer. Another issue was, at that time, MSU was one of the only universities that ran in quarters, not semesters, so I'd lose credit if I transferred schools. When my mom gave me that exercise, all those concerns faded away in favor of what my heart and soul guided me to do. I'm forever grateful to my mother for teaching me this technique and supporting my decision when I needed her support.

When my dad returned, it was too late to change my mind and return. He had a few colorful French words before shouting, "Ma fille, qu'est-ce que tu as fait?!" ("My little girl, what did you do?).

Several amazing things happened from following my intuition, which I had no idea would happen. We quickly found another student who needed an apartment to take over my lease (your closed door could open one for someone else). I finished at a smaller university where I lived at home, saving on board. I entered a degree program I was more enthusiastic about. The class sizes were smaller (twenty-thirty, not three hundred). I was to build relationships with my professors and students in the same program. I returned to the ballet studio, where I thrived and worked as a student teacher. My grades vastly improved. While I lost credits and took another year to graduate because I lived at home, it wasn't as expensive as MSU. The best part? I felt like myself again.

> "You're braver than you believe,
> And stronger than you seem,
> And smarter than you think."
> **~A.A. Milne, Winnie the Pooh**

I never considered myself "psychic," but I refined my intuition, studied with many excellent spiritual teachers, and learned many tools besides the foundational tool my mom taught me. I've shared this tool with friends, managers, coworkers, and clients. I used my intuition in my corporate job, building teams, creating new programs, and understanding what motivates my clients. There were dozens of great examples of wonderful things happening. The missteps occurred when I ignored intuition or my ego took over. Making decisions based on "a feeling" you have or ignoring logic or at least conferring with it first can be scary. But inspired intuition can fuel a sound plan and give you the patience to see it through. I've seen many examples of fantastic outcomes of people who made decisions based on intuition after sorting out others' opinions.

A former colleague and friend I have coached for years used the technique after a job layoff. She was a single mom who urgently needed a job. She was interviewing for two jobs, the first of which was close to giving her an offer. She wasn't as excited by the first job as the second, and she'd have a 50-minute commute each way. The interview process took longer with the second job. When the first offer came through, I suggested she try my mom's tool. When I asked her how she felt, she said, "She had a feeling about the second job," even though she hadn't received an offer yet. She held out for the second job and got it. It was more money and close to home, and she has thrived at that company for seven years.

Another friend was laid off from her senior executive position a few years ago and had a choice to make. She could have gone to work for another company, but she wanted to start her consulting firm. She went with her heart and, in the first year, made more than she earned in her former job.

I have friends whose college-age children decided against college. They followed their hearts and took up a trade. One helped build a thriving organic brewery, and another taught themselves coding, eventually leading to them running a developer team at a financial company. They are very successful and, more importantly, happy.

In addition to career directions, I know people who found all kinds of things, such as homes, partners, pets, and artistic pursuits, by following their hearts.

Imagine what life would be like if people didn't have different talents and didn't follow their hearts. It would be boring.

We love watching great entertainers, sports figures, influencers, and anyone good at their work. They make what they do look effortless by tapping into innate talents. While inspirational, they can't replace your unique soul. What they have is the ability to tap into their intuitive inspiration (and some luck). We don't need to aspire to be "stars" to be happy; we can just be who we are and follow what's meaningful.

You are a brilliant, magnificent soul. There is no one else on the planet like you. Plug into your light and see how powerful you are! It's simple once we learn what is "ours" vs. what is "someone else's."

"Simplicity is the ultimate sophistication."

~Leonardo Da Vinci

It was by guiding a friend that I found my life's purpose. How could that be? I've spent my career in media and data sales and marketing. I discovered that I was using my intuition and coaching people outside of work. I weave my intuition into everything I do. It's about intention. I used to think I was thinking outside the box—until I realized it was more than that. I can see the heart of an organization and my fellow humans. Although very different, the theme is the same: intuitively bridging the gap between ideas and their application in the physical world. Whether serving others with healing energy and intuitive coaching or delving into the pulse of an organization, my intuition takes center stage. I hope this tool resonates with you.

THE TOOL

Decisions can have consequences, so planning and saving money might be necessary before you leap. Practicing patience is much easier if you follow something that lights you up. If you're newer to this, I advise building this muscle by starting with small, inconsequential decisions like what to wear and what to eat for dinner, etc., then working your way up to more significant decisions. Learn how these decisions "feel" in your body and know how to trust your guidance. This tool is simple and widely available. Some could call it a "meditation." I don't call it meditation because some people I've worked with run in the other direction at that suggestion, saying, "There is no way I can sit for hours with my eyes closed; my mind is chaotic and won't shut up."

Think of something you're having difficulty deciding (remember to keep it simple first).

Sit quietly for a moment. Close your eyes. Try to forget the decision for a few minutes.

Take a deep breath for five counts, hold your breath for seven, then breathe out for nine.

Then, think about your question. What is the first answer that comes to mind? That is the answer. How does it feel in your body?

If it's hard to decide, do something physical before the breath exercise. Walk, run, clean the house, whatever distracts you. Then, go back and do the exercise. How does it feel in your body?

I know I'm on track, especially with tough decisions, when I feel a sense of ease or relief in my solar plexus and the middle of my chest.

As you practice, you'll get to the point where you will trust that you will automatically know it's telling you the answers.

I hope this simple tool is helpful. Know that there is always support if you need it. May you be blessed and enjoy your journey connecting with your intuition!

Kristin is an intuitive healer and coach. She is a Certified Master Professional Coach, Usui Reiki Master, and Jikiden Reiki attuned. She has a B.A. in organizational communications and effectiveness and a B.A. in metaphysics. Kristin combines her intuitive healing talents and formal education in her coaching and healing practice to help people elevate their talents, transcend challenges, and navigate life and professional transitions to live more authentic, meaningful, and abundant lives. With a 24-year professional background in media and marketing, she also leverages her expertise and intuition to help executives and companies build more collaborative organizations, develop go-to-market strategies, and improve the effectiveness of salespeople and between product, sales, and marketing teams. Kristin's clients have successfully moved through complex divorces and job layoffs, made meaningful career transitions that more closely aligned with their souls, achieved job promotions, and navigated challenging spiritual awakenings.

Connect with Kristin:

For a free consultation, visit her website:
https://www.creativeclaritysolutions.com/life-coaching

CHAPTER 5

THE MOMENT YOU ZONE IN

Empower Yourself with Mindfulness to Avoid Fear

By Lisa Attanasio, MSW

MY STORY

All dressed up with nowhere to go. I never thought this would be the case. Thanks to COVID-19, it is. My husband was an essential worker, my daughter was in class online, and Coco and Bella, my toy poodles, were sleeping. Wow, I feel good today and am ready to tackle the world. The problem was that the world was practically closed. The gym was closed. Nordstrom, my favorite department store, was closed.

"If you need me, I'll be surfing the internet!" I was sure everyone heard me. I'm pretty sure the neighbors heard me as well. *Eh, why not? I'll just start a business. I have time!*

"Honey, you can't just start a business. You don't have a business degree or know anything about the nuts and bolts of how to do it. You need a website and web design knowledge, and I don't think you even know what search engine optimization is!"

Bless my husband, but he wasn't looking at the big picture, and while he believed in me, he couldn't think outside the box. He'd come around later on, but I decided I was indeed going to do this. I believed in myself. I read countless stories about people finding themselves during this trying time. I made up my mind and would go all out!

I had to create my brand. From an early age, I knew I had a special ability and was ready to start my journey. While I was happy in my life, I wanted more. I needed more.

I started by enrolling in several online courses and advanced my ability as an evidential medium and psychic. I practiced doing readings while educating myself, just as an athlete has to train in their sport. My work is never 9-5, and there was no time clock to punch in or out. The more hard work I put in, the more successful I'd be. I wanted my work to be fulfilling, and I needed to give back to the world. I was ready to surrender to the universe. I had my trusty computer, my beautiful desk, and a cozy office my husband built for me. I developed a website, all while continuing to take classes. I meditated daily while doing medium and psychic readings for my friends and family. Wow, things are going great! I felt like a shop owner in a little town who had just hung a sign stating they were open for business. But my confidence quickly changed to doubt. *How are clients going to find me? Am I going to have enough clients to flourish?*

What the heck am I doing? I can't do this. I have no clue how to get clients. I don't even know where to start. Am I crazy for doing this? I should stop before I get in too deep. Maybe my husband was right; I don't know what search engine optimization is.

As I fell backward in my early endeavors, my husband caught me. He was my rock and the person who believed in me more than anyone. His warm smile and gentle hug made me feel better and safer. I wanted those hugs to last forever. I almost succumbed to doubt and fear. "Listen, Lisa, I don't know the logistics or timeline, but I know you got this. You have overcome so much in your life, and I will not stand here and watch you question yourself," he said. This empowered me and gave me back the confidence I needed.

He was right. I could do this, and I would. I might not have all the answers, but from that moment on, I was determined to forge ahead, leaving doubt in the rearview mirror.

I had my website up and running. I advertised on Facebook and started putting up posts on positive affirmations and mindfulness, all while doing some professional evidential medium and psychic readings. I was happy and content. Things were moving along, but I couldn't help but feel I was missing something. I couldn't quite grasp it, but something was lacking.

Come on, Lisa. Think girl! Deep breaths.

I realized that I was an individual with my own style and needed to stop comparing myself to others.

Just do your thing. Trust in the universe.

I decided to examine my goals and take things to the next level. I've always known we're not alone and that Spirit is always with us. However, not everyone understood this. I communicated with Spirit from an early age, and I was now training in this ability. I was becoming more confident and was ready to level up and get out there!

I did most of my early readings over the phone via FaceTime and Zoom. I then traveled locally to psychic fairs, starting with a chair and a small table. I looked at each fair as a success. I grew and became more confident in my abilities. However, one should never be too comfortable, as that can lead to complacency. I was not about to rest on my laurels. I wanted to expand my business and reach out to help as many people as I could. I was not going to sit back and be satisfied.

I performed a small demonstration at a local store and did some psychic and medium readings while my daughter set the mood with uplifting music. We had pens, notepads, and business cards in little goodie bags on the table as I tried to promote my business. I don't sell a product or something tangible. I perform a service. I realized that being authentic was part of how I'd be successful and build an excellent reputation.

You must be authentic in everything you do, as reputation and word of mouth matter. I've been verbally attacked and called horrible names by people who don't believe in what I do. And then there's the issue of how some psychics take advantage of clients who may have just lost a loved one. They prey on that grief. It's horrible and hurtful, but I'd be naive if I didn't acknowledge that they were out there. I've learned why integrity matters.

A genuine, well-trained psychic with integrity wouldn't predict the future for someone, and because of these charlatans, I have to accept that some people will never be satisfied with a reading. Criticism is sometimes harsh.

That client was demanding and doubted everything I said, but I had to keep calm and keep going. Nothing was going to derail me.

I would not allow the seed of doubt to be planted. I believed in my ability, trusted my intuition, and did not worry about external factors. I don't fear the future because I am living in the moment and zoned in. You need confidence to overcome fear, and there are powerful ways to gain that confidence. Let's explore one now.

THE TOOL

A Practice for Empowerment

Become empowered using the following steps: set your intention, breathe, use imagery, and stay mindful in the moment. Utilizing this method will help you avoid going into fear mode.

We need to believe in ourselves and be confident. While blind faith isn't always wise, it's still important to feel sure of yourself. The universe will respond to your positive energy and vibration.

The first tool is setting your intention. This step helps us see a positive outcome even if we're unsure about the nuances of getting there.

The following tool is breathing and getting into a positive state of mind.
The third tool consists of imagery and, in a way, seeing what we're working towards.

Finally, putting everything together—zone in and be mindful of staying in the moment.

It's human nature to doubt; we can utilize doubt as a safety check in some ways. However, it can wreak havoc on what we're trying to accomplish in life.

1. Set Your Intention

Start by sitting in a comfortable, quiet, serene room. It can be in a chair or on the floor. You need to be still. Let your body relax. Close your eyes. Breathe in and out slowly. You will know when you are in a relaxed state. You're now ready to start setting your intentions. Think about your success. Send out positive thoughts to the universe. I ask the Divine to help me develop trust in myself. Show gratitude for what you have, such as a house and a wonderful family. Spend a few minutes in this state of mind and just picture things going your way. There is no specific endpoint, and each person has a unique way of doing it. There is no cookbook for setting your intention. You will start to feel empowered and ready to start your daily journey.

2. Breathe

Breathing is something we can control. You should now be in a positive frame of mind and be ready to breathe deeply. Start to become aware of each breath. Feel your diaphragm elevate and descend as you breathe in and out through your nose. Hone in on your slow inhalations and drawn-out exhalations. This technique will activate your parasympathetic nervous system. Your body will further relax, and we can move on to imagery.

3. Use Imagery

Use your imagination and emotions to see a vivid picture of your success. Sometimes, I picture myself on a beach on a quiet summer day. You can visualize yourself in a beautiful garden surrounded by flowing flowers. This breathtaking backdrop sets the tone for things to come. While this may seem vague, it's the stage where we can see our new business bustling and humming along. If you own a cafe, for example, start to see patrons sitting at tables, chatting, reading magazines, and drinking coffee with their muffins. If you're in online retail, picture the number of website hits going up and up. You can see the number of website hits mounting. These images in your mind will be different from person to person. You'll soon realize the images will also differ daily for you. While you may have tangible goals, the idea is to observe the big picture. You'll feel the excitement while working toward your goals. Keep the momentum and focus while deflecting negative thoughts, which can quickly derail you. The last technique we use will keep us in this fantastic moment and ward off worry.

4. Stay Mindful in the Moment

You should now be in peak condition, raring to go. It will take effort and practice to get to this point. It's far too easy to get ahead of yourself and jump into something without being prepared. We're not designing these techniques to settle everything on day one of your journey. Instead, they will help move you along to your destination. Cultivating mindfulness and staying in the moment is the culmination of everything discussed thus far. We must avoid worrying about what might happen in the future while not dwelling on the past. Imagine yourself in a white bubble. It's warm and bright and will shield you from negative thoughts. This bubble is your protection. The outside of the bubble is a mirror and shield. Defeatist and pessimistic thoughts will reflect or bounce off you. Being in the moment is a state of mind, and you're on your way to learning how to achieve it. People will continually ask how they know when they are in the moment. You'll just know. You'll quickly begin to recognize it. Mindfulness is beneficial not only in the business world but also in many aspects of life. Many tools for success are akin to a recipe written in narrative, but no two people travel the same path.

Let's Get the Journey Started!

Hard work and dedication are crucial for getting a business up and running. You have to trust in the process. At some point, doubt and fear will inevitably start to seep into your day. You're safe. Use the tools we discussed to fight back. If you worry too much and constantly send negative energy to the universe, you will hold yourself back. You can overcome these hurdles and stay on track. Remember to use your toolbox. Believe in yourself and what you're doing. Set the intention and see it happening in front of you. Don't get overwhelmed and realize that few things worthwhile happen overnight. You're not competing with the store next door or the online competitor. You're competing with yourself. You are in control of your thoughts and mindset. Don't overanalyze things. Despite all this, we will occasionally find ourselves living in fear. Armed with a fantastic attitude and beaming with positive energy, you will prevail and reap the benefits of all your hard work. Believe in yourself and keep smiling. The universe has a way of figuring out the rest.

"Optimism is the faith that leads to achievement. Nothing can be done without hope and confidence."

~Hellen Keller

Lisa Attanasio, MSW, owns HeavenlySoulandSpirit and is a professional evidential medium, psychic, past-life reader, and animal communicator. Lisa also performs demonstrations and has been featured on television, podcasts, magazine articles, and online instant readings. She is tutoring students in evidential mediumship and is certified in spiritual healing by the Spiritualist National Union. She has trained with exceptional tutors like Tony Stockwell and Sharon Harvey and is a part of Soul Journey Sundays.

Lisa spent many years as a social worker and uses this background in her empathetic work. She also was an essential part of a local women's shelter.

Lisa created a vision and devoted herself to Spirit, culminating in a fulfilling and prosperous business that she is so proud of. Now, she's ready to share her knowledge and authenticity.

Connect with Lisa:

Website: https://heavenlysoulandspirit.com
Facebook: https://www.facebook.com/HeavenlySoulandSpirit
Instagram: https://www.instagram.com/heavenlysoulandspirit
Bestpsychicdirectory.com: https://bestpsychicdirectory.com
LinkedIn: HeavenlySoulandSpirit
The Morning Blend TV Appearance: http://bit.ly/3E3RxIN

CHAPTER 6

I GET BY WITH A LITTLE HELP FROM MY GUIDES

How to Receive the Answer to Any Question

By Becky Dotson

MY STORY

No matter how intuitive someone is, we can all get stuck in our human ego brains, especially if we're seeking intuitive guidance on topics we're way too emotionally connected to.

This book is filled with some really amazing tools to help you tap into your intuition! My tool is going to be a little different because it requires a little help from those on the other side or what I like to call spirit guides. And while I call them spirit guides throughout this chapter, you can use angels, God, passed loved ones, or whatever feels good and true to you.

Even as a psychic medium, my intuition can get a little hazy if I'm too emotionally attached to something. In my case, I struggle to tap into my intuition or listen to my higher self when it comes to romantic relationships. This is just for me, but for others, it could be career, familial relationships, money, etc.

I drove myself crazy whenever I dated someone new. My mind raced with questions: *Does he like me? Is this going to work out? Is he the one?* I couldn't sit still for two seconds to listen to my intuition no matter how hard I tried (thanks ADHD and attachment disorders!).

I spent 100s if not 1000s of dollars on psychics to tell me what they saw about

51

whoever I was dating at the time. Then, when the relationship inevitably ended (like my intuition tried to tell me, but I didn't want to listen), I went back to those same psychics to ask why the relationship ended and what was wrong with me. It's important to note here that I was not a practicing psychic or even that into spiritual stuff at this time in my life.

Then, in 2019, I went through a very traumatic breakup. We dated for a few months, and in the beginning, I thought, OMG—this is the one. This is why it never worked out with anyone else.

We never fought, he was constantly showering me with love, affection, and gifts. He wanted to spend all of his time with me and we couldn't get enough of each other. I thought things were perfect until three months into the relationship when everything started to fall apart.

About two weeks into our third month of dating, he withdrew all of his attention, affection, and love, and I couldn't understand why. While he never did anything blatantly concerning, I couldn't shake the feeling that something wasn't right, so I decided to confront him about it.

"It seems like you've changed, and you've been pulling away. What's going on?" I asked.

"This is all in your head," he replied. "Nothing has changed. We're fine."

And for two more weeks, I tried to believe that was true. It got so bad I started to think maybe I was crazy and began to ask myself, *do I need to see a therapist? What did I do wrong to make him pull away?*

But after two agonizing weeks, I felt nothing had changed, and things still felt distant between us. I decided to end it and was devastated. I started asking myself questions: What did I do wrong? Was he going to come back? Why did this happen to me? I couldn't understand why this seemingly perfect relationship fell apart.

Over the next week, I fell into a mini-depression. I couldn't get off the couch. I stopped doing things I loved, like going to the gym and hanging out with friends. Personal hygiene went out the window. And I could barely take care of my dog. After a week of this behavior, my roommate decided she had enough (I can't blame her; I probably smelled so bad). "I think you should make an appointment with my life coach," she suggested. "She also happens to be a psychic."

I never really heard of a life coach, but I knew I liked psychics, and to be honest, I would've done anything to feel better. I scheduled an appointment right away, and for the first time in a while, I was excited about something. *Maybe she can give me hope, maybe even some answers. Maybe she will tell me he will come back and that he misses me as much as I miss him.* I mean, I was used to psychics telling me what I wanted to hear about my past heartbreaks, so why would this be any different?

But this psychic was different. She didn't give me many answers at all. She told me, "You're a gifted psychic. You will use your gifts one day."

Funny enough, I brushed that off and said, "Yeah, maybe I am a little intuitive, but what about this guy? Is he going to come back? Is he heartbroken? What should I do?"

"Well, I'm seeing that he does this to everyone, so it is best to let him go, work on healing yourself, and if he is meant for you, he will come back," she replied.

"Um okay, but is he going to come back? Is he heartbroken? What should I do?"

I said, clearly not ready to receive the message.

She hesitated and then said, "Ask your spirit guides to show you who he is."

"Ask who to do what?" I had no idea what she was talking about.

"We all have spirit guides who are here to help us on our life journeys. Ask them to show you who he is, and I promise you will get clarity," she clarified.

"Uhhh—okay," I muttered.

As I hung up the phone I was frustrated at the lack of immediate clarity. *Why can't she tell me more; isn't she psychic?* I just want an answer!

A few minutes later, I calmed down and could digest what she suggested. *I guess I have nothing to lose here, so I might as well ask.*

I said out loud, you know, to make sure they could hear me, "Hey guides, universe, spirit, whatever you call yourselves—show me who Mark is. But please send me three distinct signs."

I felt like asking for three signs would up the ante, and I liked the number, so I just went with it.

Sign 1- What is a narcissist?

Fast forward a few nights later. I was still totally bummed over the breakup, and I kind of forgot about my question to my guides. I was at a bar with one of my best friends, James, when Mark started texting me out of the blue.

I think I may have reached out to him. I don't remember a lot about that conversation, but I do remember James reading the text messages and saying to me, "Becky, this guy is a total narcissist, and he is manipulating you."

"No, he's not. You don't even know him," I snapped back. James could tell this was a sore subject and so we left it at that.

When I got home that evening, I Googled the term "narcissist" because, believe it or not, that was the first time I ever heard that term, and I had no idea what it meant. And I was too proud to ask James what it meant, so I got to Googling and went down a complete rabbit hole. As I read more and more about narcissistic behavior, I saw similarities in Mark's behavior. However, the more I researched, the more confused I became.

It was clear I was still way too emotionally invested to see things clearly, so I asked again, "Okay guides, I'm still not convinced; show me two more signs."

Sign 2- Anonymous Sender

A week went by after I discovered what a narcissist was, and I still felt down about the breakup. I recall deciding to take my dog, Ollie, for a walk to try and get out of my funk. As I began to walk, I felt my cell phone buzz in my pocket. When I went to check the message I was shocked at what I read.

It was a number I didn't recognize. "I know you are going through a difficult time with your break up, but you're better off. Narcissists don't change."

I was in complete shock, and my mind started going a mile a minute.

"Who is this?" I managed to reply.

"I am one of his exes. I don't want to tell you which one because we're all scared of him, but I thought you deserved to know."

I didn't say much more after that. To be honest I thought it was very strange that his ex would even know who I was. We only dated for three months and I never met many of his friends or family. It kind of creeped me out enough that I didn't know what to think.

But there was that narcissist word again. *Maybe my guides are trying to tell me something.*

"Okay, guides," I said. "I am a slow learner here; show me one more sign."

Sign 3- Broken Ski's

A few days went by since I received the mysterious text, and I have to admit, I did a little more research on this narcissist term. I went down another Google rabbit hole, and some pieces of the puzzle came together.

He always talked very poorly about his exes, and "poorly" puts it nicely. Every girl he dated was crazy or cheated or was crazy and cheated. He showed up at random places I was at with my friends, and I thought that was sweet and romantic and that he really liked me. The thought that he might be a tad bit controlling went right over my head (ahh, to be young again). He would make over-the-top displays of affection followed by withdrawal of affection for no reason or to "punish" me. Everything was in my head or my fault, and he took no personal accountability.

The more I read, the more it made sense but I still wasn't convinced. That was until I received my third sign from spirit.

It was a random Saturday afternoon when I walked downstairs to my kitchen and grabbed my cell phone from the charger. As I looked at my phone, I noticed I had a text from James: "I was at the ski shop yesterday and I saw Mark with some girl."

Again, I was shocked, and I replied as fast as I could, "How do you know it was Mark? You've never even met him?"

"I remember seeing him on your Snapchat stories; I know what he looks like, and someone at the store called him Mark."

"What are the chances the same Mark is at the same ski shop 40 minutes from your house in Maryland?"

"I don't know, want to grab some lunch?"

"Ugh, fine. Pick me up in 20."

Honestly, I didn't really want to go out, but I wanted to know more. I did think it was interesting that my best friend was at the exact same ski shop where Mark used to work over a decade prior that was 40 minutes away from where James lived.

In addition, Maryland is not known for its skiing. Crab cakes and beer, absolutely, but skiing? Not our thing. So what are the chances they were at the same ski shop on the exact same day?

At lunch, I just could not wait to ask, "So, are you sure you saw Mark at the ski shop?" I blurted out.

"Yeah, I'm pretty sure it was him. I remember him from your Snapchat stories and he was with some girl."

"Okay, well, it could have been his mom or his sister," I snapped back

"She told the sales rep that Mark was her boyfriend."

"Well, we don't even know if it was my Mark; maybe it was some guy who looked like him. I mean, what are the chances?"

"I knew you were going to do this, so I took a photo."

"Show me now!" I said as I snatched his phone from his hand.

My mouth dropped; I couldn't believe it. It was Mark and his ex-girlfriend.

The one he said was crazy and cheated on him. Not to mention, he was already back with her a mere month after we broke up. In that moment I intuitively knew he used me to get her back. Another thing I read that narcissists do—they use people to get what they want.

At that very moment, I was done. I was finally over him. I deserved better than someone who would treat me like that, and I now understood I was being saved.

Thank you, guides, for showing me who Mark really was. Wow, this stuff really works.

Ever since that day I have never hesitated to ask my guides for a little extra intuitive guidance. And I always use my rule of three method. I have used this when I had an opportunity to move to Boston then again when I moved to Colorado. I have used it with angel numbers because I am constantly seeing them.

For example I will see 555 and ask my guides to send me that angel number two more times within the day if it's important. If I see that number two more times, I will look it up and take the first definition that pops up. To no surprise, the message is always exactly what I need to hear at that moment. I've even looked up the same angel number on different days and have gotten different definitions.

No matter how much I work with them, I am always impressed by how they manage to show me signs. I love hearing stories from my clients who've used the rule of three method when needing advice from their guides. I hope this tool serves you and helps you cultivate a strong relationship with your own guides because sometimes you just need a little help from the other side!

**All names have been changed to protect identities.

THE TOOL

The Rule of Three Method

Step 1:

Ask your guides any question you wish to receive intuitive guidance on.

Step 2:

Ask them to send you three signs (optional: you can put a time limit on it).

Step 3:

Be open to the guidance even if it's something you don't want to hear.

Becky Dotson, also known as the dog mom medium, is a practicing psychic medium who helps deliver messages of clarity, guidance, and love from spirit guides and passed loved ones on the other side.

As a compassionate and gifted psychic medium, Becky serves as a bridge between the spiritual and physical realms, providing guidance, healing and connection. With five years of experience honing her intuitive abilities, Becky offers insightful readings, channeling messages from loved ones, spirits and the universe. Becky's mission is to empower individuals on their life journeys, fostering self-discovery, comfort and transformation.

Connect with Becky:

Website: https://www.dogmommedium.com
Instagram: https://www.instagram.com/dogmom_medium

"Make your search for the Light your most fueled flame. One day you will awaken to the awareness that you are already there. In the Light you will hear a tone, and you will find a passage."

~ **Cher Lyn**

CHAPTER 7

QUANTUM PRESENCE TECHNIQUE®

Your Doorway to Business Success

By Liz Goll Lerner, LCAT, LCPAT, LPC, ATR-BC

MY STORY

How often do you ignore your first whisper of intuition? Fighting it away with logic, fear, and predicted outcome.

How often, in hindsight, do you wish you had paid attention to that whisper? How many life or business decisions have you looked back on and thought: *Wow, if I'd only listened to my gut? If I'd only listened to myself instead of what I believed I was supposed to do. If I'd only not been afraid.*

Do it NOW. If you don't, you will never fulfill your life purpose.

The voice was clear, deep, and crisp while simultaneously having no tone but a depth that seemed to reverberate over eons.

The drive from the airport was several hours. *What a beautiful state! It's getting wilder. Thank goodness it's the next turn. Whoa, it's a dirt road.*

After driving up the long and rocky dirt road surrounded by forest on each side, the view opened up to a wide grassy expanse. A large, inviting main cabin was at the top of one of the hills. Small cabins popped into view between the trees. Awesome, a pond and huge decks. *I'm in the right place. Everywhere I turn, the earth is calling me.*

I traveled to a spiritual retreat. Why that one? Why now? This time, it wasn't the topic calling to me; it was the land. I saw the description of the location and immediately thought, *I'm going. I must be on that land. No question. I have no idea why, but I know I have to go.*

For decades, I meditated, learned energy work, studied spiritual practices, created rituals, and led programs and retreats, incorporating knowledge about multidimensional realities and esoteric teachings into my work as a transformational coach and psychotherapist.

I took all I learned, paired it with my clinical training, and translated it into everyday language and clear actions to assist my clients' understanding of their true inner voice, barriers to listening, and how to heal and bring themselves into balance to make aligned, high-level practical choices so life could hold more joy and comfort than sorrow and stress. Now, it was my turn.

I studied great teachers and watched peers become spiritual teachers, and often thought, *I've known that information in my bones my entire life, yet I am not on a big stage. I don't have a special guide. Maybe this lifetime, I'm meant to work quietly in the background. I'm helping people find their light and true essence. That is enough.*

I was in for a surprise. When I arrived and met the proprietress, there was something mystical about her. Even so, she was inviting and approachable. She was the host of the retreat center and, for me, the unexpected bonus.

As I settled in, I had a conversation with the proprietress, a teacher in her own right, about my belief that I was to be a quiet guide in this lifetime. *This is so cool*, I thought, *I can actually talk that way here.*

"Why don't you go out to the deck near the pond and feel the energy? Try out the meditation cushions below the giant crystal," she said.

This was a special place, one that buoyed and accelerated one's ability to elevate oneself exponentially. It felt like ripe fruit on a tree, ready to be picked. So, off I went to the deck, never thinking for a moment that my belief was really about keeping myself small.

I came back, "Okay, I feel it. The energy here is palpable. I know I'm here for a reason. I don't think I have a guide, and I want to know if I do. How do I find out?" Now, it probably sounds crazy after decades of work and meditation to think such a thing. We all have something guiding us, whatever we want to call it, and I have felt guided. Every time I connected with my higher self and asked for guidance before a client session, every time I asked the same for myself, I was guided. But the question lingered.

"Go back out and ask," she said. So, I did. It turned out I did have a guide whose name I didn't recognize, and through many communications both with the proprietress and my guide, I was secure in knowing that this was real and trustworthy. I could use this new tool to ask my most burning question.

For many years, before the retreat, I focused on staying in my marriage in support of my child and, in all fairness, my concern about making it on my own without local family support.

I went back out to the deck and asked, When can this be over? When is it time to leave? *And the resounding voice said, Do it NOW. If you don't, you will never fulfill your life purpose.*

I was freed!

It took another year and a half to carefully put all things in place. Through that process, I created the Divorce Well and Thrive® method that's now helping countless individuals transform their relationships with clarity and compassion for all family members.

At the core of this work is The Quantum Presence Technique® (QPT®). When doubt, fear, insecurity, or unhelpful behavior patterns appear, stillness is needed—stillness with a purpose.

I carried a lot of additional stress that created a barrier to my business growth and creativity. We humans can hold a lot of stress and still function. To be at optimum performance and joyful at the same time, we need to drop the unnecessary self-talk, overthinking, worry, and old patterns that don't serve us. It all takes energy, and when we're using energy for worry, we're not using energy for our good.

John, a CEO, came to me for executive coaching. The problem? Even with all his expertise, when he presented to an audience, he became wooden. As the new leader, he had many speeches scheduled in front of thousands of people. One might think a speech coach or lots of practice would've done the trick, but it didn't.

We met and discussed his problem. John decided to hire me for my two-and-a-half-day LGL Accelerated Breakthrough Coaching® Intensive. We began. "I don't fully understand what this is or if it can help, but I'll try anything."

In the first part of the day, we explored what he experienced while presenting to an audience and connected these feelings to his life story. We reached a deeper understanding of the blocks to embodying his new position and what prevented him from being free and easy on stage. We talked about identity in leadership, relationships on his team, and how he saw himself transitioning his self-view as he entered into greater leadership.

Experiencing this newness and weighed by some old concerns, John wasn't free to be fully himself. When there is worry or fear, we're no longer using the logical or strategic part of the brain that showcases our gifts the way we need to in critical situations. Instead, we're immersed in fight or flight. Survival is the goal. As mammals, we flee, fight, or freeze. All are detrimental to John's situation and unconsciously appear in tone or body language.

Next, I taught John part one of QPT®—how to become still in the body and how to recognize when thoughts were overtaking him. "I can feel it. I can feel myself leaving my body when I start getting scared," he said. "When that happens, I can't remember, I can't be me! I go into the tunnel, and I think I'm failing."

The next step was learning how to find true balance and peace while staying in the body and connecting with the heart—being able to say, "I am okay in this moment," out loud and mean it.

When John mastered that, our focus was on purpose: his vision for what he wanted to communicate and why–the key.

"I can't believe it! I can do this! This was so complex and yet so simple. I am so grateful."

John was able to step back, find himself, and, in the moment, choose where he was putting his attention. He chose his purpose, not his fear. He was an absolute star in all his speeches and meetings.

The connection between my story and John's is that the real gift is realizing that:

1. We're never alone, and the right wisdom comes to us when we most need it.

2. The answers are always in our heart of hearts. When we can see the forest for the trees the answers are crystal clear. We can take the right action.

3. Self-doubt, as strong as it may seem, with all the seemingly supporting data, is just an illusion.

The way to finding your perfect guiding source isn't as difficult as you might imagine. Join me in opening your doorway to what is hiding in plain sight.

THE TOOL

The Quantum Presence Technique® is the roadmap to our own sacred doorway. It roots us in the body so we can expand beyond our wildest dreams, all the while being clearheaded, making decisions and choices using all the information we can access. When we're present, moment to moment, we're not blown off course by our emotions or fear-based thinking. Instead, we're standing solid and connected to the Earth, in our bodies, connected to life force, connected to the heart, and being inspired by love-wisdom. We can connect to our sublime guidance—the key to personal freedom, abundance, prosperity, and our next simple or complex inspired choice.

When we expand what we believe is possible, more of the world opens up to us.

The Quantum Presence technique has three steps. Today, you will learn Step One. It's the cornerstone.

Tips For Success

If meditation or being still makes you uncomfortable, please check with a health professional before adding this or any new technique to your repertoire.

When feelings arise during this exercise, please do not ignore them, try to destroy them, or eradicate them. The exercise is about using your abilities to recognize and place them in the proper time, place, and perspective. It is about identifying them and even honoring them by appreciating that more work may need to be done to understand why they're showing up or what needs to be healed. But, most importantly, it's about stepping back from a difficult feeling you may be experiencing in a particular moment so that your best self can make appropriate choices and shine through.

QPT® involves the body, the mind, and the breath.

The Body:

Why is it important to be in your body?

Our body has cellular memory. When we think back on something distressing that occurred or that we are worried will occur, there is a physical experience that goes along with it. Sometimes, people ignore it. Often, they don't make the connection that our bodies play a big role in navigating whether or not we can let go of suffering.

Have you ever taken steps toward change only to see the effectiveness quickly diminish? The reason it doesn't work in the long term is that the body was left out of the equation.

The Mind:

You may have heard the expression "emotion follows thought." It's true. Where you put your attention leads your heart and body into suffering or into balance. It can also lead you into joy.

The Breath:

Our breath takes us into the present moment. When we consciously focus on our breath, not only does it still our wandering thoughts, it also re-vitalizes us. Breathing consciously reminds us we are alive and that there is more to us and to what surrounds us than our thoughts.

Have you ever noticed that you stop breathing when there is a stressful situation? No breath equals no flow, no presence, no choice.

The Technique: Let's begin!

This step can be done on its own at any time. It's necessary whenever you need to come back into the now, into your body, into the room, into a conversation that you had checked out of because it was uncomfortable or because your mind wandered. Practice is the key.

When first beginning to learn and practice the Quantum Presence Technique® QPT® you may close your eyes to concentrate. The ultimate goal is to be able to do this with your eyes open in any situation.

Choose a place to begin that is private, feels safe, and where you will not be interrupted for about 15-20 minutes. In the future, you will need much less time to successfully employ this technique, but pacing is critical during your first experience. Continued practice will help you perform this technique more quickly. It will eventually become second nature.

Note: Some people are visual learners, and some are not. Some people are tuned into the sensations of the body; some are not. Any instruction, visual or physical, can be accomplished just as easily with your intention. In other words, don't worry about doing it right. Trust that you are.

Find Your Feet

The simplest way to get into your body is to find your feet and breathe. Your eyes can be open or closed. If closing your eyes makes it hard to balance, use open eyes with an unfocused gaze.

1. Stand (if able) or sit in a chair supporting your spine, your feet touching the floor. Standing allows you to feel the full weight of your body being supported by the floor.

2. Take a deep breath. Put all your attention on the sensation of your feet connecting with the floor.

3. Focus on the floor supporting the weight of your body, and breathe, putting all your attention into your feet. Imagine the breath is moving directly to your feet and all of your concentration is on the sensation of the bottom of your feet against the floor. Your feet may feel tingling, heavy, or gluey as you focus on connecting your feet to the floor. When extraneous thoughts arise, return your attention to your feet.

4. Breathe deeply, exhaling any stress that needs to be released.

5. Imagine the floor as the earth. Every breath moves vital energy into your feet, up your legs, into your torso, and up into your arms, shoulders, neck, and head.

Your body knows exactly what to do; you are simply becoming conscious of it. Every time you breathe, your body is taking in nourishment and letting go of what it doesn't need. You are revitalizing every cell, muscle, tendon, and organ.

6. Standing tall or seated in your chair, imagine a string connected to the top of your head that is gently pulling you into an upright position. Imagine breathing in through the top of your head, often referred to as the crown chakra. Imagine energy flowing through you.

7. Take a deep breath and put your hands on your heart—one on top of the other.

8. Feel the sensation of the breath moving your chest.

9.   Visualize a sun of golden light in your chest/heart center. Allow it to grow with every breath. Allow the golden light to fill up your body, brightening every cell, muscle, tendon, and organ. Imagine your skin glowing with golden light.

10.   Ask your heart—not your mind—am I okay in this moment? Then listen. With intention, let your thoughts drop down into the heart so the heart and head are connected. Ask again and listen.

The answer is yes.

If you have chosen a safe and quiet place to do this exercise, your body knows that you are safe in that moment, even if you might feel uncomfortable. You are physically okay. Our emotions often take us into fight or flight, an ancient reflex meant to protect us from harm. In this moment there is no immediate danger to your person. Your emotions are playing tricks on your mind. Trust your body.

How do I know I am in my body? Thoughts aren't swirling, emotions aren't roiling; you are standing, feeling your body, aware of your breath, feeling your feet connected to the floor, and that is all there is.

If you ask yourself if you are okay in this moment and the answer isn't yes, then your thoughts are continuing to feed your emotions. Start again by breathing and putting all your attention on your feet.

This sense of being okay is an aspect of knowing, not of thinking.
So, What Now?

You've become present, connected to your heart, and you know you are safe. Now, choice comes into play. If you experience emotions or troubling thoughts, keep bringing yourself back into the body. Choose. Where am I putting my attention? What is my alternative choice?

With your hands on your heart, practice listening. Practice discerning what your mind is saying versus the wisdom of the heart-brain. Your body knows the difference. The body is the secret force, the heart is the hidden doorway, and your mind and heart connected brings the highest form of wisdom. Love/wisdom is the most powerful change-maker, the purest guidepost.

Total access to love is the key to solving the deepest problems. The roadmap to clearing our deepest hurts, changing the patterns of old wounds, and finding a way to heal and transform. New ways of being take shape and change lives for the good.

This technique brings you to the access point.
Step in.

The result will be your best business decisions and glowing personal moments.

Liz Goll Lerner, LCAT, LCPAT, LPC ATR-BC, is the founder of Enlightened Communication Institute® and the owner of Your Inspired Choices®, LLC. She is a transformational coach, psychotherapist, art therapist, author, communication expert, spiritual teacher and artist.

Throughout her decades of experience, she has been a true pioneer who developed many highly respected, groundbreaking psycho-educational and therapeutic programs for her own practice and health centers across the nation. She was an adjunct professor at George Washington University and played a pivotal role in a longitudinal study focused on public health for the NIH through Georgetown University's Center on Health and Education.

With certifications in mindfulness practices, energy medicine, and bioenergetics, Liz uses multiple modalities in all aspects of her work. Her unique approach is influenced by her deep understanding of the more subtle energies of the body and archetypal psychology. Above all, Liz is committed to creating an integrative, whole-system approach that helps every type of client meet their full potential. She is the creator of Enlightened Communication Through Luminous Living®, which transforms the way individuals and organizations interact and communicate to help them achieve their goals in even the most high-stakes situations.

The Quantum Presence Technique®, the tool highlighted in this chapter, was first published in Liz's new book Divorce Well and Thrive® Your Guide To Being Your Best Self Under The Worst Circumstances, Balboa Press, 2024.

Connect with Liz:

For information regarding training in the full Quantum Presence Technique® **email:** info@yourinspiredchoices.com

Websites:

https://Enlightenedcommunicationinstitute.com

https://yourinspiredchoices.com

https://DivorcewellandThrive.com

LinkedIn: https://bit.ly/42vuLno

Instagram: https://www.instagram.com/accounts/onetap/?next=%2F

Fcebook: https://www.facebook.com/inspiredchoices

My book, *Divorce Well and Thrive*: https://bit.ly/3CrAL62

"Know thyself."

~ Inscription at the Temple of Apollo at Delphi

CHAPTER 8

BODY AND SOUL INTEGRATION

Live Life Guided by Your Divine Wisdom

By Dana Theresa, RN, MPH, The Metaphysical Mentor

MY STORY

Like most personal odysseys, I experienced a loss that ignited action toward my purpose. In my case, the thing I lost was my vision.

My experience with visual impairment helped me see the valuable role body and soul integration plays in guiding our lives. Here's how my journey to connect my body and soul began.

It was my last semester of nursing school at the University of Illinois in Urbana-Champaign. Buzzing around our apartment, I gathered my binders and half-written patient care plans and deposited them all into my green backpack. The smell of coffee brewing urged me to hurry up. I wanted to down a cup before heading to my clinical rotation at the local mental health center. That was until my roommate, Carrie, cornered me in the living room.

Half joking and half frustrated, she asked me, "Do you want to move to California with me or not?"

I buried my face in my hands. "Oh, man! I'm sorry. I can't decide. I still need to think about it."

Carrie presented me with this opportunity over a month ago. At that point, we were both exasperated with the topic. I laughed at my indecision hoping to soften the mood.

Carrie got that look on her face. She furrowed her eyebrows and scrunched up her lips, trying to read my thoughts.

"Okay, whatever. But you need to give me an answer soon. I'm not going to ask you again."

Damn. She's serious. I do owe her an answer.

"I know," I said, attempting to placate her. I stood up taller to meet Carrie with her sternness. "I'll have an answer for you by tonight."

This seemed to satisfy her for the time being. Carrie slung her maroon backpack bulging with nursing textbooks over her shoulder, grabbed her travel coffee mug, and headed out the door.

I stood there in our living room, stunned and overwhelmed.

How am I going to make this decision?

Anxiety flooded my chest, and my mind started to spin.

Carrie was my best friend in nursing school. Graduation was getting close. We were about to step out into the real world. Carrie had it all figured out. Her boyfriend graduated a semester before us with a degree in engineering. He landed a job in Pasadena, and Carrie planned to move there with him.

When Carrie asked me to come along, I knew we'd have a blast together, but something held me back.

I always assumed I'd move home to Chicago after graduation. That's where I grew up and where all of my family and friends were. That would be the easy choice.

But is it the best choice for me?

Until this point in my life, I had a dark, dirty secret. Dysfunctional family drama and unhealed trauma waited for me back home. At the root of it all was this:

My mom has schizophrenia.

She was hospitalized with her first psychotic episode when I was four years old. No one in my family ever spoke about what was wrong with her. I didn't fully understand what her psychiatric illness was until I figured it out for myself in nursing school.

I'm a highly sensitive empath, and I grew up with a family that never talked about their feelings. I took on the guilt, shame, and grief that everyone around me felt with my mom's condition, and I deeply suppressed my own dark and painful emotions. At the age of 22, I didn't tell anyone about my mom's illness. The relationship with my dad was strained and detached. Still, I coveted my relationships with my siblings and my friends back home. No one in my immediate or extended family left Chicago or even traveled outside of Illinois. I felt a sense of responsibility to move home.

How can I leave Chicago?

Yet, the opportunity to move to California enticed me. I could start over. Leave the past behind, as they say. I'd never been to Los Angeles, but I knew it had sunshine, the beach, Hollywood, and palm trees.

I can move there, can't I?

As I stood in the living room of our college apartment, a sudden determination took over. I had to figure this out.

What if I "feel" into these two choices instead of obsessively overthinking them?

I closed my eyes. I brought my focus inward. I felt into a future life back home in Chicago.

It looked dark. I saw heavy gray clouds. There was a contraction in my abdomen and a sick feeling in my stomach. Moving back home to Chicago felt, well, icky.

Hmm. That's interesting.

Then I switched to California.

What will my life be like there?

The clouds parted. I saw sunshine and a rainbow. A sensation like joy poured over my body. There was an energetic opening in my chest. My lips curled upward in a sweet little smile.

I guess I'm moving to California.

That was all I needed to feel. My body gave me the answer. That night I told Carrie I was moving there with her.

Some might say I was running away from my problems. Hell yes, I was. That was what I needed to do at that point in my life.

I absorbed all of the heartache and shame of my family. I gave my power away to my mom and her illness, trying to fix her. I felt abandoned and rejected by my dad. I didn't know who I truly was.

In that moment, I discovered my Divine wisdom as it spoke through my body showing me what my soul wanted. It wanted a new experience. It wanted me to leave Illinois so I could find my truth and start to put myself back together.

My move to California changed the trajectory of my life, and very soon after I arrived there, my healing journey began.

Now, let's dive deep into how souls work, shall we?

Every soul is a fractal of the Divine. Since we all have a soul, we all have Divine wisdom.

Your soul chose to come to Earth at this time for a reason. That reason involves learning lessons that expand your consciousness and support your soul's evolution.

Inhabiting a physical body is a requirement for your soul to have a human experience on Earth. Your body is the vessel for your soul. They're not separate. They're deeply intertwined and connected.

Your soul needs a way to communicate with you. It needs to give you validation when you're on the right path. It also tries to redirect you when you've strayed from your life's purpose. One important way your soul speaks is through your body.

Your soul is energy. Therefore, your soul's language is energetic. Just as everyone's body is different, your soul may choose to communicate with you in special and unique ways. It's up to you to decipher how your soul talks to you. If you want to continue your soul's evolution in this lifetime, it's also important to listen.

Learning to listen to your soul is an ongoing process.

Six years after my move to California, I ended up in the Rocky Mountains. I transitioned from bedside nursing to a management position at a hospital in Vail, Colorado.

Now, my job entailed reviewing patients' charts and implementing quality improvement projects. Turns out I had a knack for this kind of work. However, soon, I realized my soul was calling me into something different.

I was training to become a Reiki Master. The desire to transition to a career in holistic healing burned inside. I daydreamed about quitting my job and starting my own business as an energy healer, but fear and scarcity mentality were holding me back. I had a well-paying job with benefits.

How can I leave it? It's safe.

Later I came to realize my thinking mind overshadowed the subtle sensations of my soul. The excitement and passion I felt around starting my own business as a Reiki Master wasn't enough to overcome my fear of stepping into the unknown. My soul needed to give me a stronger nudge in the right direction.

After two years in my quality improvement career, I was diagnosed with fundus flavimaculatus. Try saying that five times fast. It's a macular dystrophy, which caused my central vision to be a little blurry. There was no treatment to correct it. Still, the ophthalmologist told me it was a stable condition. I breathed a sigh of relief and continued with the status quo. I wasn't paying much attention to the energetic feedback coming from my body.

A couple more years passed working my desk job at the hospital, and I continued to suppress my passion for holistic health and energy healing.

Then, a funny thing started to happen. My eyesight got worse. Reading the computer screen was a challenge. Dark spots made it hard to see signs, read books, and recognize people's faces. Something wasn't right. I needed my eyes checked again.

Sitting in the exam room at the University of Colorado Anschutz Eye Center in Denver, I stared at the visual acuity chart several feet on the wall in front of me. The familiar antiseptic smell I was used to as a nurse lingered in the air. I took some deep breaths to calm my nerves, but a heavy sensation burrowed into the pit of my stomach.

I can see the giant "E" at the top of the chart. But everything else looks like a big fuzzy mess!

I chose to see a different ophthalmologist this time. He already examined my eyes and left the room to review his findings. The giant "E" and I continued our face-off until I heard a gentle knock on the door. This time the doctor had two medical students with him.

Uh oh. This is going to be a teaching moment for all of us, isn't it?

"Dana, we've reviewed all of your tests and exam results," the physician told me. "You have Stargardt's disease."

"Oh-no!" I exclaimed. I covered my face with my hands and immediately began to sob.

I didn't even know what Stargardt's disease was, but it sounded bad.

The doctor handed me a tissue. The medical students stared at the floor and shifted their weight from side to side.

I pulled myself together the best I could as the doctor explained it to me. In a nutshell, Stargardt's disease is early-onset macular degeneration. With this condition, photoreceptors in the eyes die and fall off leaving the affected person with blind spots in their central vision. Usually, the peripheral vision isn't affected.

In most cases, vision loss happens slowly and then progresses more rapidly before it levels off. There's no treatment.

My mind raced as the doctor spoke.

I don't want to go blind! I'm too young to lose my vision! How am I going to ski, rock climb, see the faces of the people I love, and travel the world?

My dream life flashed before my eyes as if saying to me, "Good-bye! This is never going to happen!"

Just like the photoreceptors in my eyes crumbled and fell off, my world was demolished into a pile of rubble. I left the doctor's office in a state of devastation.

Some say the ancient oracles were blind because the strength of their inner knowing transcended any need to see with their physical eyes. I decided it was time for me to embody my inner oracle.

After the initial shock and grief settled, I came to a powerful conclusion. I didn't want to waste any more time sitting behind a desk reviewing charts in a job I wasn't passionate about. Deep inside, I knew this eye condition was happening "for me," not "to me."

I was not "seeing" myself or my path forward clearly. I was not perceiving how divinely gifted I am, nor was I acknowledging all of the power and potential I had to completely shift into the career of my dreams.

When I think about the intelligence of my soul and how it communicated to me through my body, it leaves me awestruck. Through manifesting this eye dis-ease, my soul powerfully nudged me in the direction of my purpose. My soul was not about to have me stay in a desk job I wasn't meant to be doing anymore.

It was my soul's way of saying, "Come on! Let's do this already! It's time to stop messing around and step into your passion! That's what you came here for, remember?"

I knew I had to listen to my soul, so I took the plunge.

I left my full-time career as a nurse and became an intuitive entrepreneur. I am forever grateful to my soul for pointing me in the right direction.

It is up to you to learn the language of your soul. If you don't listen to the whispers, your soul's messages get louder and louder. In Earth school, if your soul finds itself off course, it will use your physical body to get your attention.

So how do you decipher the language of your soul and listen to the energetic messages it sends through your body?

I'm about to teach you in a beautiful and fun way.

THE TOOL

In five simple steps, you can begin the process of Body and Soul Integration.

Step 1: Set the mood.

The first time you try this, I highly recommend you pick someplace quiet where you will not be disturbed. Turn off any excess noise like the TV or music. Remember, the messages your soul sends through your body are subtle, so it is important to create a supportive environment for you to receive them.

Step 2: Ground and come home into your body.

Find a comfortable upright seated position. Close your eyes. Feel the Earth's energy beneath you and soften your body. Take three slow and expansive breaths. Using deep breaths is an easy way to anchor into your body and land in the present moment.

Step 3: Quiet your thinking mind.

Notice if the thinking mind is still active. Do you have lots of thoughts swimming around, or does your mind feel calm and receptive? If your thoughts are taking over, let them release, dissolve, or float away. If the thinking mind is still not at peace, try this:

Bring your focus to the center of your forehead. This is an access point to your third-eye energy center. It's the home of your intuition or your Divine wisdom. Keep your focus there for several breaths, and observe the present moment.

Now here comes the really fun part!

Step 4: Feel your soul's positive response.

By this point, you're in a relaxed state, and your soul has the opportunity to speak to you through your body.

Ask your body to show you what your "YES" feels like.

Notice what happens. It may be subtle. The sensations you feel are not to be judged or critiqued. Simply observe how your body tells you "YES." If you don't notice something the first time, try asking the question again. There is no right or wrong answer. Everyone's body and soul language is different.

Step 5: Feel your soul's negative response.

Next, ask your body what your "NO" feels like. Again, take in and notice the energetic response you receive. Generally, this will feel very different and perhaps the complete opposite of a "YES."

Step 6: Trust.

This step may be the hardest part. Usually, what gets in the way of trusting and implementing your Divine wisdom is your thinking mind. If you notice yourself judging, worrying about, or over-analyzing the energetic feedback you received from your soul, it's your thinking mind trying to take back control. Pause. Take a deep breath. Simply tell the thinking mind to relax and send it some love. You can always take a break and repeat the process if you want to confirm your "YES" and "NO" body sensations.

For example, my soul's "YES" feels like an upward movement of energy from my heart center to my third eye. Often, a smile comes to my face, and the energy feels uplifting and positive. A strong "YES" response gives me the full-body tingles.

My soul tells me "NO" with a downward heavy sensation from my forehead to my gut. A strong "NO" can even make me gag or feel a wave of nausea.

How to integrate your Divine wisdom into your life.

Just like a muscle, the more you use your body and soul integration, the stronger it will become.

Now that you know your soul's positive and negative energetic cues, you can practice using them in your day-to-day life. Start using it for small, easy decisions like "Do I want a smoothie for breakfast? Or oatmeal?" You don't always have to come into a deep meditative state. Take just a few seconds to close your eyes and tune in. See how your body responds to each option, and go with the one that feels like the positive response.

You can work up to using this tool for bigger life choices like "Will being a co-author of this book support my personal growth and business expansion?" My soul gave me a resounding "YES" by the way.

Beautiful soul, we are here on Earth navigating our human experience. Sometimes you may forget to listen to your Divine wisdom. That is completely okay. It's a way of being that you'll grow into with practice. The more you integrate your body and soul, the more aligned and expansive your life will become.

Peace and Love,
Dana
P.S. Here's a link for you to practice your Body and Soul Integration with me:
https://youtu.be/wdEy9l1xqoQ

Dana Theresa, RN, MPH, The Metaphysical Mentor, guides conscious leaders and healers to transcend their life obstacles so they can elevate their impact within the world. From a nurse working in hospitals around the United States to a public health advocate volunteering with Doctors Without Borders in Uganda to becoming the CEO and Founder of her holistic healing practice in Vail, Colorado, her life's work unites Western and Eastern models of health and wellness.

Dana is a Board-certified holistic nurse with a Master of Public Health. She is a Reiki Master, Registered Yoga Teacher-200, Akashic Records Practitioner, and shamanic healer. These modalities come together in the transformative energy work Dana offers for those seeking deep levels of holistic healing and Universal connection. She serves as a mentor for healers who desire to take their practice to the next level. The work Dana offers is not merely a technique; it's how she has transformed and continues to live a magical life.

With the mountains of Colorado as her home, Dana loves to ski powder, bike tour, rock climb, connect deeply to nature, and wander all over this beautiful planet.

Connect with Dana:

Website: https://www.danatheresa.com
Facebook: https://www.facebook.com/danatheresastar
Instagram: https://www.instagram.com/danatheresastar
Email: dana@oehealing.com

"To gain the Kingdom of Heaven is to hear what is not said, to see what cannot be seen, and to know the unknowable–that is Aloha."

~ Queen Lili'uokalani of Hawai'i

CHAPTER 9

PSYCHIC PORTALS

Accessing Spiritual Realms for a Blissful Life

By Kazemaru Yukawa, Certified Evidential Psychic Medium

MY STORY

On a warm sunny morning, with a gentle breeze caressing my skin, I sat by my meditation altar on my lanai and stared into the empty void of my soul.

I don't know what to do. It is like I lost my soul. The needle of my spiritual compass is spinning out of control, directionless.

Nothing felt quite right ever since my closest friend, soul sister, mentor, and colleague, Raylene Ha'alelea Kawaiae'a, passed away suddenly in a car accident up north on the island. Our shared mission, once so clear, shattered into a thousand pieces I couldn't gather.

I stopped running our retreats, I could no longer hula, and life seemed to scatter further—people I once trusted and gave my all to revealed behaviors that broke our connection. Soon, I went through physical and hormonal changes as well, adding to the chaos, and somewhere, I thought my state of being could be fixed medically.

For years, I did not recognize myself and sought help, going to doctors, therapists, naturopaths, and acupuncturists. They all held me with compassion and care, preventing me from falling. I took endless tests, supplements, and hormone replacements, desperately hoping for relief. Yet nothing worked enough to restore my spirit.

I meditated since I was fourteen and had a vibrant life; this was the first time my spiritual practice offered no solace, answers, or relief; it was the first time I was spiritually lost.

Sitting by my altar that morning, I surrendered. I let everything I was, everything I thought I knew, dissolve. I let it all go, allowing myself to slip into the vast, unknown valley of despair.

I remembered Raylene used to say, "Ask the Source when you have a question, and the answer will come. That is the Hawaiian way to be. Ancestors will come in your dreams and prayers to talk to you."

My gaze fell on a photo of Brahma Baba, the founder of our meditation school, arranged on my altar alongside a photo of Raylene and an incense bowl from my late father.

Out of the ether, I heard a warm yet direct voice say,

"You have to go and see a psychic."

A psychic? I don't know any psychics here; I don't know what to do with this information.

But the voice lingered, nudging me on as I listened to the comforting sound of one of my roosters crowing in the yard.

Meant to be?

Later that week, I had appointments in Honolulu and looked for a psychic online. I picked one and called,

"Could I please book an appointment?"

"Yes, but there is a six-month wait."

My heart sank a little.

As I was getting ready to head to the airport, someone called from their office,

"Do you still want to come? We just had a last-minute cancellation."

I canceled my flight and was soon on my way to Lan Vo's office.

Her house, nestled beside the Pali Highway, was cool, clean, and quiet. The smooth marble floors beneath my feet felt grounding, and the air buzzed with intense anticipation.

I booked the appointment under a different name to ensure nobody could research me. Yet the moment I sat down in front of Lan Vo, she asked no questions but knew deeply personal details—the names and nationalities, locations, and situations of me, my friends, and my family.

"Stop giving so much to everyone; they never give back to you. Don't give everything you have for free, including money; they take, take, take."

"But I never see it coming," I replied, not expecting an answer.

"Don't worry; they will naturally disappear from your life because of the protection of your pure heart. You don't need to do anything."

Lan Vo sounded like a concerned mother. She accurately pinpointed some of the struggles I had been going through in detail, with a couple of names. Her words reverberated through me.

It is funny, yea, how I don't use my intuition regarding friends and constantly think everyone has the best intentions.

At one point, in a sweet voice, she sang a line from a song someone wrote to me back in the 80s:

". . .The only way to get through to you. . .love la la. It was in a movie, remember?"

Well, it was a movie called Stockholms Natt, and I had to go home and search online because I had forgotten all about it. Yep, she was right about the lyrics, ha!

My background is pretty obscure, so I recognized her exceptional ability and knew I could trust her. She laid out my secrets and struggles and made my answers clear. It felt like dark, heavy clouds finally dispersed from my thunderous sky, and I could feel the sun's warmth on my soul again.

Toward the end of the session, she said something that changed everything:

"But you are a psychic too; why did you stop? You helped so many people using your psychic abilities—like a doctor. You need to get back to it."

These words were like a spark that ignited a fire within me, a flame of motivation to reclaim and use my psychic abilities for the greater good. It was a fire that realigned me with who I am spiritually. I could see why I had not functioned and felt broken, as I had tucked away the way I naturally navigated life.

"I don't know how. Can you teach me?"

"Yes, come with me to Vietnam, and I will show you everything."

Stirred by Lan Vo's words, I began extensively researching valid psychic teachers as I was not ready to travel to Vietnam. That is how I found Tony Stockwell, the renowned British Medium of Street Psychic and host of the British TV series *Psychic Detective*. I recognized something pure in him. Soon, everything aligned with divine timing, and Tony became my mentor.

This alignment brought everything back in flow as if guided by a benevolent power from beyond.

One early September morning in class, Tony gave me a reading. Unexpectedly, with no information from me, he brought through my friend Raylene with vivid, undeniable detail. And as if having received a call from the heavens, he said,

"She has a message for you, Kazemaru. She wants to see you rise and fly, saying it's your turn now. As you journey through the years of your life, she hopes that you will be just like her and more. You will heal and hold many and make people feel seen. And she will work through you like a guardian angel for all the days of your life."

When Tony finished, I turned off my Zoom camera, warm rivers of tears streaming down my face.

I knew she was around me, but this—what profound comfort of confirmation.

After that reading, shadows of doubt lifted. I felt the reality of what Hawaiian aunties used to say: "Nobody ever dies; they just change address."

A Love Link Never Dies.

After two years of daily training, I offered sessions for a minimal fee. One of those early readings convinced me that this was my path.

Stepping out of the hot shower in the morning and preparing for the session, although I'm in Hawai'i, I look out of the window and see the vast planes of Africa with unfamiliar trees and bushes in a dry landscape.

When drying my hair, I wanted to put it in a traditional African yellow and green headscarf. As I don't have such material, I put my hair up in a bun, which I never do for a session. Twisting strands of my hair while working relaxes me, allowing information to flow better.

The sweet fragrance of the gardenia I just picked makes me dreamy. As I get ready, I feel relaxed.

I request my booking assistant never to give me any details about clients, only their first name. I had no information but a sense of what was to come.

As I turn on Zoom, a young man introduces himself:

"Hi, I am Ossie from Sweden."

"Aloha, thank you for the trust in reading for you. It's nice to meet you."

But when I breathe in and connect to his soul, clear images flood my mind, and the lovely face of a woman, obviously his late mother, emerges beside his face.

"I know you said you are from Sweden, but I see your small family home somewhere in Africa close to the sea in a city starting with the letter L. Sorry, but I also am aware of scenes where your controlling father gathers the kids and takes you all away from your mother, never to return."

"Yes, that's what happened, and the city is called Lomé," Ossie confirms.

I have never been to Africa or heard of Lomé, but the information came vividly because his mother's spirit strongly wanted to connect with her son.

The scene before he was taken away emerges as well, and I blend with the spirit of his mother, a strong, simple woman who loves her children profoundly but is helpless under the force of her husband.

Even though the young man in front of me is now a grown-up, I see him around six years old or younger.

Blending with his mother, I feel the urge to put him on my lap and feed him with my hand a dish of rice and beans in tomato sauce and a very particular-smelling spice similar to berbere.

"I don't know this dish, but I want to feed it to you. Do you recognize this food?"

"Yes, I know the dish. We ate it often, and it was the very last dish my mum fed me before we were taken away from her when I was around six," Ossie replies.

After all her children are gone, I see her walking to a buzzing market, exotic to me but not too far from her home. The air is filled with chatter and conversations. As she gets veggies, she tells everyone about her beautiful children.

"My children, I am so proud of them; they will do very good," I hear her say as my chest swells with a mother's selfless love. In my heart, I feel her hope that they will have a better life wherever they are now.

"Ossie, this love keeps your Mama going, even though she never sees you again."

Ahh, this makes me cry bittersweet tears just by remembering it all.

A few weeks later, Ossie returned for a second session, and I felt the rush of joy in my chest from his beautiful African mama.

"Finally, I'm talking to my beautiful boy again. Tell him how proud I am of him," I hear her voice eagerly in my mind.

"I want to ask her what she thinks I should do as a career," Ossie says.

As I listen to her mind, I hear words from my mouth say;

"You would do good in work like IT, but not just the technical side. You are so good with people you should do communication or coach people in the field."

At this point, Ossie lights up with a big, radiant smile and says, "Then I am on the right track because that is exactly what I do."

His mama's confirmation provided comfort and reassurance. By the end of the session, his face was calm, and his energy was more centered.

Ossie's mother's love flowed so strongly that it filled me too. Even though I don't have children, I felt the tremendous strength of a mother's love through her.

Something changed in me. My commitment to reconnecting souls through mediumship grew, and I felt a new respect for a mother's love. Oh, and the dish she fed her children—I regularly cook it now and feel her love every time.

Can you imagine the comforting feeling of knowing that your long-lost, late loved ones are aware of you and your life, even if they are not with you physically?

Why portals?

Psychic mediumship can be a portal between realms, providing comfort and healing on a spirit level. It reassures us that the love bond of spirit is strong enough to survive death, distance, and life's dramas because we are all eternal spirits.

Those in spirit can also reach out to us, guide us, love us, protect us, and provide what we need.

You can access psychic portals in many ways, such as through dreams and visions, the arts and other people, or by visiting sacred locations.

Ultimately, portals allow us to touch the unknown and be embraced by universal love so we can be all that we are supposed to be.

We're all surrounded by boundless, timeless spiritual love and can increase it by connecting to the Source and the life force flowing through our universe and our very existence.

Reconnecting on this level is a thing of bliss.

Working in the subtle realms has shown me that life, at its core, exists to nourish and support us with love. If we're ready to embrace it, we can live together in the spirit of Loving Aloha—a state of being that connects us to each other, spirit, nature, and the Source itself.

> "Healing is primarily healing of the spirit, not only the body.
> To learn healing is to learn the spirit of aloha."
>
> **~ Raylene Ha'alelea Kawaiae'a**

You can learn to access a heightened state of awareness so that you may find bliss on your path in life.

THE TOOL

Here's a tool to enter psychic portals by developing your extra-sensory perception.

Preparing

Collect a pen and paper. Sit comfortably, relax, and breathe deep into your lower belly. Breathe deep yet natural and easy, letting the airflow flow without strain. Gently bring your attention to what thoughts trickle through your mind; observe. Do not force them to stop; thoughts are a tool for navigating your life.

Observing

Observe what images and impressions are related to the past, present, and future. Write down the three categories, place your thoughts in the category they belong to, and let them stay on your paper.

Centering

Center your focus on the core of your being, sensing a glowing light, the eternal life force of you. Let energy rise from within, knowing your existence is much more expansive than you can imagine. Feel as if your body dissolves, sitting in your eternal form.

Getting ready

Cut a sheet of paper into six pieces. Draw an image on each piece—stars, circles, flowers, numbers, anything simple—or use a stack of cards. Turn the cards face down, shuffle them, and spread them before you.

Close your eyes briefly and gently feel your soul's energy.

Practicing

Please open your eyes, move your hand over the pieces, feel them, and stop randomly to touch a card. Don't use your mind or imagination.

What image comes into your mind? Turn the paper. Did you see the right image? Repeat until you do.

Trusting

It is crucial to surrender your mind, trust that your spirit knows, and allow your hand to move naturally without consciously getting involved. Your meditation practice helps you enable a quiet mind.

Connecting

You can also get a stack of playing cards with simple images or numbers and use photographs of people you know, in spirit or still here. Shuffle and repeat the practice.

You may notice that when you feel drawn to a specific photo of someone, they might suddenly contact you, or if they have passed away, a song they loved will play.

Integrating

Integrate this practice into your daily life with variations, like sensing the hometown of some random person or driver you chat with and can confirm.

Or, waiting for an elevator and there are five or more options, let your body move to where you feel the next elevator will arrive.

When someone gives you a gift, see what's inside before you open it.

Sit with a friend, let them focus on a color or an animal, and then tell them what you sense or see.

These are all things I did when I was younger.

Develop your intuition while entertaining yourself. Gradually, you'll end up in the right place at the right time, see events before they occur, and hear whispers of guidance.

Trust.

Find what aligns you with who you truly are.
Let the invisible currents of spiritual love lead the way.
Go with that love, and your life will flow and be magic.

Keep your inner flame lit and walk through psychic portals to your bliss!

Aloha!

Kazemaru Yukawa is a Certified Evidential Psychic Medium who apprenticed in meditation, spirituality, and healing arts from a young age under great masters in Japan, India, and Hawai'i. She also trained in psychic mediumship with international teachers.

She started Zen Meditation at age fourteen at her father's martial arts dojo. From age twenty-four, she apprenticed under a Sensei in healing arts in Japan for six years, then worked professionally for many years.

Kazemaru lived full-time at an ashram in London, UK, and India for ten years, teaching meditation and spiritual lifestyle. She also ran a meditation center in Tokyo, Japan. She was invited to teach in Hawai'i, where she is based.

For the last twenty years, she has focused on learning Hawaiian spirituality through chants, hula, and traditional Ho'oponopono. She learned spiritual principles from Hawaiian elders who naturally walked with one foot in each world.

Kazemaru trained for many years to certify in evidential psychic mediumship, remote viewing, and trance mediumship and also does pet communication.

She offers individual and group readings online and in person.

When Kazemaru is not working, she enjoys stand-up comedy, gangster movies, snorkeling, losing herself in Hula and Hawaiian music, visiting friends' cacao farms to taste their exquisite dark chocolate, and talking to animals.

Connect with Kazemaru:

Website: https://kazemaru.com
YouTube Channel: https://www.youtube.com/@KazemaruPsychicMedium
Instagram: https://www.instagram.com/kazemaru4u
Facebook: https://www.facebook.com/Kazemaru4u

CHAPTER 10

THE POWER OF INTUITION

Trusting the Path of Spirit

By James O. Joseph Jr., The Unintentional Psychic

MY STORY

A little over a year ago, September 16th, 2023 (strange that I remember the exact date), it seemed like any other day at the office since January 2021. I had one of four small offices on the main floor of a renovated two-story house known as the Adirondack Healing Center, a collection of practitioners who work within metaphysical modalities or tangents. Suites 1 and 3 had been empty for months. Suite 2 was my Reiki Master's office. She is a massage therapist who practices several other modalities. She convinced me to take an office in the building to start my Reiki practice, seeing something in me I still hadn't found.

So much has changed. I grew my Reiki clientele without stepping into the psychic mediumship skills I'm now known for in the area.

June had a steady business with her growing service menu and a big dream. She talked for months about opening up her day spa and blowing life into her vision. I've always been a big fan of anyone with a big dream. So many people are terrified to dream big and allow themselves to believe it can happen. I genuinely support anyone who dares to embrace the path less traveled.

Many times between our client sessions, we stood around chatting about many things. On this day, casual as can be, she simply says,

"I am moving out of the building. I will open my day spa in the next month or so."

As she stated this, so many things instantly went through my head. Of course, I was happy for her; we had built a solid friendship in the couple of years I was there, and I knew she was a master manifestor who could achieve anything she wanted. She was the building manager; *who will fill that row now? Will it be me?*

The most significant for me was the image that popped into my mind's eye as soon as she finished telling me her news, like she flipped a switch or pulled a time trigger. It was fast but crystal clear. More clear than any other vision up to this date. As of 2019, I consciously came to terms with some unusual skills I possessed that became unavoidable—my psychic and mediumship abilities. I was still trying to understand their development, the processes, symbols, and determining when information was from spirit. I'm still regularly creating the manual as I go, leveling up on symbolism, expanding my general connection, and realizing new tools within my abilities. It's like graduating from grade to grade in school, building the new on top of tested and true previous understanding.

The image is simple but detailed. Picture it: I'm standing just a foot away from a window, looking out. The sun, beaming in, kisses my face, warm and welcoming. I'm focused and looking out over a courtyard with a building to the left and right. It's simple, not elaborate. A vivid collage of flowers and greenery is right outside the window.

I never saw the image before and didn't know if it was a real place or anywhere near me. *My only thought was, am I moving too?* More times than I can count, the image popped into my head at the most unexpected times, always leaving me asking:

Am I moving offices?
Is this a real place?
Where is this place?

This went on for almost two weeks.

I normally drove home from the office the same way every time, straight up a main road in the area, and by this point, I'd driven back and forth thousands of times. But this time was different. Before I knew it, without a thought, I turned left into a drive I'd never once looked at, pulled into a parking spot, and stared ahead, not a thought in my head. My mouth was wide open as I gaped at a small office compound of three simple facade buildings surrounding a grassy courtyard. To say I was shocked is an understatement; to be in a place that has always been there but to never notice or be drawn to in the fourteen years I've lived here simply blows my mind. The process that got me there still blows my mind.

I took the whole experience as a sign: *this is meant to be.* If I hadn't had other more minor, unusual experiences in the past couple of years, I would've been unhinged. I contacted the leasing agent to show me what was available, which we did the next day. I knew it was the next step. The whole experience was so in my face it couldn't be denied.

For an hour or so, we proceeded to walk through and discuss the details of building 1, both suites A and B. The realtor talked about the leasing terms, rent, insurance, etc. The building was a bit rough and had obviously been empty for several years. What really caught my breath was the rental fee, which you would've never noticed by looking at my external calmness. The rent was at least five times what I was paying for the space I had currently, not even to mention utilities, WIFI, etc.

I knew it wasn't the right building. In my vision, I looked out the window of Building 2, suite A.

"Is that suite available?" I asked.

"There is an engineering firm in there right now. They are moving out at the end of the year."

"Oh, okay," I said.

I knew if it was any of the spaces, it would be 2A, but. . .

Where will I get the money for rent and deposit? How will I continue to pay the rent?

It simply was not realistic at that time. I was doing well but by no means had a booked-up work schedule. I grew organically. What am I to expect with just going full-time in January 2023?

I stepped away from the experience, knowing I followed through with what spirit gave me. I was open to the messages and symbols. I was willing to follow the breadcrumbs, taking one step at a time, knowing this whole experience was definitely something more than me. At this point, there seemed to be no next step. In my head, the money was a serious roadblock and simply did not exist. Even if I did have the money, how would I get Jeremy on board? So I went about my life.

Soon, my Reiki Master moved out of the building. I was alone there most of the time, working my client schedule, growing my business, and looking forward to Thanksgiving and Christmas. It was the first holiday season in years where I was not beyond stressed creating gift baskets and gift designs for a gift shop I had run for years and closed the previous November.

The holiday season did not disappoint. It was calm, relaxing, and peaceful. I was dedicated to leveling up my business for the next year, expanding my brand, and growing my clientele. I used the last week of December to make a rough calendar of classes, events, and collaborations for 2024 to focus on where my life was going and maximize my potential. I had a solid plan and felt good about the new year. I felt I could make some real progress in 2024.

It was Friday, January 12th, like any other Friday. It was not a full day, but everything was moving along. My cell phone rang, and I picked it up, seeing it was my landlord. *I don't think I have talked to Bill since the day I signed the lease in 2021.* There was never a need on either side.

I picked up, "Hi, how can I help you, sir?"

"Hi James; as you may have noticed, I have been struggling to get the empty office spaces rented out for a while now."

"Ya, it's been some time since someone has been in them," I replied.

"You have been a great renter, never an issue, I am grateful."

"Thanks, I am glad to hear it," I said.

"But I've decided to turn the main floor into apartments. There should be no issues with finding tenants for them. I hate to do this to you, but I need you to move out. The sooner the better; I will give you up to 30 days if you need. I would be glad to give you a letter of recommendation if you want. I would like to start the remodel work as soon as possible. We will possibly start work in the common areas as soon as next week."

"Oh, okay," I replied, not knowing what else to say.

"Thanks for being so understanding." He hung up.

Most people would've gone right into panic mode. For a brief second, it felt like the rug was being pulled out from under me. I just leveled up my commitment to this growing venture, trusting in a spiritual purpose.

As soon as he hung up, as clear as day, I heard don't. When I heard it, it was not like hearing from outside your ears, but the back of your head, behind your ears. It sort of sounds like my voice, but not. This is what I now know as my psychic hearing, which does channel in on occasion.

Don't!
Don't tell anyone.
Don't think about it.
Don't worry.
Don't panic.
Just sit on this.

That's what I did, which wasn't an easy task. I'm an emotional person, and a situation like this would normally have me running to my spouse, but not this time. The message was so authoritative, so supporting, and so in control I simply trusted. Several times over that weekend I almost blurted it out to Jeremy. He was leaving early Monday morning for a work trip, but I did what Spirit said.

Sunday Morning I woke up with the thought already in my head:
Is suite 2A empty?

I hadn't thought about the office compound in weeks, believing it was a hard stop. That day I had a couple of errands to do around town and decided to stop into the complex. I was so self-conscious but knew none of the businesses there were open, so I got out of my vehicle and looked through the windows of suite 2A. There were desks, chairs, and filing cabinets, but anything that would signal a functioning business was gone.

I connected with the realtor, and we walked through the suite the next day. He covered all the same issues he touched on months ago when we met. Once we walked through, I quickly realized the floor plan was ready for move-in without any construction. The money was still a sticky spot, but for whatever reason, I was not paralyzed by it. I had more than enough for the deposit and the first month's rent. I had already come to terms that I'd be subleasing, and there was no resistance from the landlords. The big problem was that I had no one to sublease at the time.

The next two weeks were a bit of a blur, lots of meditation, asking for guidance, and of course, there was the issue of getting Jeremy on board. Usually, he has a fair amount to say about big moves like this. He is a Capricorn and has a solid perspective on business and money, but was very quiet on this venture. The air felt heavy at times between the two of us. At some point, I came out of a long meditation and asked him two simple questions.

"Do you love me?"
"Yes."
"Do you trust me?"
"Yes."

That was the validation I needed, and I began to really push forward with this move and give it my full attention. That must have been the sign that Spirit needed from me.

Your first two subleases will appear in the first week after signing the lease. The last week of the month you'll get your third and last sublease.

I trusted, and it happened.

I signed the lease on Saturday, January 28th, quite happy with what I managed to achieve. To me, it was a big accomplishment not only in this physical world but also in controlling the fear, trusting the messages, and embracing the unknown. Most people have this need to know the whole plan before they're willing to take one step. I found that Spirit will not give you the next step until you take the first.

I was not given long to bask in my achievements, thinking I'd moved mountains. Sunday, the following day, I was by myself, and I started to hear this playful laugh,

He thinks he is done; He thinks this was it.

Then, I was given a bigger plan for the next three to five years.

It's coming up on a year since the lease was signed. There has been so much growth in so many ways. I was in desperate need of a new office but ended up creating a metaphysical community center—The Phoenix Rising Synergy Center: Four offices, a classroom, a retail space, a lending library, and a new place for spiritual community. Overall, the center has exceeded any expectations I had throughout 2024. I'm proud to be the founder and caretaker.

As I write this chapter, I'm finalizing details and getting ready to sign a new lease for the center at 2A. In addition to that, I've been guided to expand the center. It has been a slow process, it took over six weeks to even get a formal reply back about the proposal. During that time, I barely bothered to reach out. If it's meant to be, it will be.

Now I have the final version of the new lease sitting in my email waiting to be reviewed. I'd be lying if I told you I had no fear. This is once again a leap of faith, a trust fall with Spirit. This last week has been a battle of the what-ifs. Writing this chapter right now is the medicine I needed to ground and center myself on this topic. There is still a slight chance the expansion hasn't happened by the time the book is published. Most likely, by the time you read this, I'll have grown the Phoenix Rising Synergy Center to two office suites containing ten practitioner offices, a lending library, a doubled classroom size, and a tea cafe retail space. This is not the full plan that Spirit shared with me, but it's a step forward. I continue to consciously be open to spiritual guidance and to be in service. I made an agreement years ago—if Spirit shows me the opportunity, I can't say no. It has been the simplest way for me to bypass the ego and fear of growth and change.

Are you ready to truly walk your path with Spirit? Are you ready to ignite the power of your intuition and its full potential? The tool below will start you on your way.

THE TOOL

Let's dive into an exercise that can help you tap into your intuition and guide you on your spiritual path. It's a step-by-step journey, with nothing but a quiet space and an open mind.

The Inner Compass Exercise

Preparation:

1. Find a quiet space: Ensure you won't be disturbed for at least 30 minutes.

2. Gather materials: A notebook and a pen.

3. Set the mood: Light a candle or play soft instrumental music if it helps you relax.

Steps:

1. **Grounding Meditation:**
    - Sit comfortably with your back straight.
    - Close your eyes and take slow, deep breaths.
    - Visualize roots growing from your feet into the earth, grounding you.
    - Focus on your breath and let go of any tension or distractions.

2. **Intention Setting:**
    - Silently set an intention for this exercise. For example, "I seek to connect with my intuition" or "I want guidance on my spiritual path."

3. **Connecting with Intuition:**
    - In your notebook, write down a specific question or area of your life where you seek guidance.
    - Close your eyes and place one hand on your heart and the other on your abdomen.
    - Breathe deeply and imagine a light within you growing brighter with each breath.
    - Ask yourself the question you've written down, and listen. Pay attention to any feelings, images, or thoughts that arise. Don't force it; let it come naturally.
    - Write down whatever comes to you in your notebook, even if it seems unrelated or abstract.

4.   **Reflection:**
   ○ Read over what you've written.
   ○ Reflect on how it resonates with your current situation or feelings.
   ○ Consider any patterns or insights that have emerged.

5.   **Closing Gratitude:**
   ○ Close your eyes again and take a few deep breaths.
   ○ Express gratitude for any insights or feelings you experienced.
   ○ When you're ready, gently open your eyes and extinguish the candle.

Tips for Enhancing the Experience:

- Consistency: Make this a regular practice, perhaps once a week, to strengthen your connection to your intuition.
- Mindfulness: Incorporate mindfulness practices into your daily to stay attuned to your inner guidance.
- Nature: Spend time in nature to deepen your spiritual connection and gain clarity.

The journey to connecting with your intuition is unique for everyone. Trust the process and be patient with yourself.

James O. Joseph Jr., The Unintentional Psychic, is the founder and caretaker of the Phoenix Rising Synergy Center, a unique metaphysical community center offering holistic resources, metaphysical modalities, and practitioner services. He is also a psychic medium, intuitive business coach, inspirational speaker, and Reiki practitioner.

James ran from his psychic and mediumship skills for close to 30 years until a life-changing situation happened that opened his eyes to a larger purpose in his life. Never wanting to be a "psychic medium," he finally released the resistance and is seemingly on the fast track of a spiritual path that he wasn't even aware of. Within that, he has become a skilled psychic medium, teacher, and mentor; he is The Unintentional Psychic.

His why is simple, may it be doing a reading, a healing modality, or planning and working the center objectives. His why is to help, heal, uplift, and/or support. As he says to his clients, "If I am not doing that, I am wasting your time and mine."

Connect with James:

LinkTree: https://linktr.ee/theunintentionalpsychic

"If the elders leave you a legacy of dignified language, you do not abandon it and speak childish language."

~African Proverb

CHAPTER 11

ᴧNCESTRAL VENERATION

Hear the Whispers of Your Loved Ones

From Beyond

By LèVonta White, CD(DONA), EOLD, RMT,

Light Worker

MY STORY

"She wasn't crazy, honey; she was talking to the dead." Gina, the medium we booked for our birthday readings, easily blurted.

"She could see things many of us can't, so they called her crazy. This is where you get your abilities from, and she wants you to continue to embrace those gifts."

Hearing those words flow from Gina's lips so casually left me in awe. My jaw dropped two inches from the floor.

My eyes welled with tears, and my heartbeat grew rapidly as I searched for the right words to speak. First, I had to swallow the knot in my throat.

"They said that she was a schizophrenic!" I finally broke.

Eventually, I went on to explain to Gina that I never met my dad's mother, at least not that I could remember.

"They said that she met and held me when I was about a month old, and then she died shortly thereafter."

I recalled how, over the years, my mother rambled on about how my grandmother

103

Mary was found deceased in her car in the garage and that it was deemed a suicide. In speaking with my dad about it, he never really provided me with anything concrete that confirmed nor denied exactly how she transitioned, so her death remains a mystery.

Tears streamed down my cheeks into the corners of my mouth, and my partner's hand devoured mine in comfort.

"She's asking that you lean on her as you develop your gifts. Ask her to guide you."

Oookay—how the hell am I supposed to do that when I haven't the slightest idea who she is? What would I even call her?

"It doesn't matter that you don't have a relationship with her; just talk to her. You don't have to call her grandmother; just call her Mary…"

"Mother Mary!" We both affirmed in unison, followed by a lighthearted chuckle.

She took the words right out of my mouth, literally.

My mind was blown, and I'm not easily impressed. I never told Gina I had abilities, let alone that I looked to develop them. That was classified information, as far as I was concerned.

In that same reading, I also received messages of encouragement from my maternal grandparents, Papa and G-ma. They were the grandparents that graciously starred in my and my son's life until their ascension. I knew them. But why couldn't I hear them and their words of encouragement for myself?

Our drive back home was pretty much a blur for me. My thoughts raced just about as fast as the cars on the interstate.

What does leaning on Mother Mary even look like? Where would I start?

As my eyes gazed out of the passenger window and the sounds of 90s R&B blasted the speakers of our white SUV, I felt a spark ignite in my solar plexus.

In that moment, discovering the answers to my questions became my mission.

My next order of business when I returned home was to enroll in my Reiki teachers' psychic medium development classes.

I secretly thought about doing this before the reading since they were hosted at my favorite metaphysical shop in the city.

Mother Mary was right. From the age of 14, I knew I could sense those who had transitioned to the other side.

My first encounter with the spirit of a loved one (that I can remember anyway) was with my first cousin Roni.

Roni, named Taronza at birth, was a studious and vibrant ray of sunshine. With her hair in plaits, she could be found under the dining room table of G-Ma's house, eating a snack and reading a book. If not there, she was out in nature, climbing our pear tree or enjoying a game of kickball with our neighborhood friends.

My younger sisters Netra, Roni, and I did everything together. Roni was more than my cousin; she was my sister.

At the age of 11, Roni died of smoke inhalation in our house fire a week or so before our very first spiritual encounter. The same house fire that my sisters and I almost lost our lives in. That's a story for another time.

Lying in the bottom bunk bed at my then-bestie's house, my eyes were finally in accord with what my brain tried to communicate to them since the night of the fire. I was in desperate need of sleep.

Heavy and dry as the Atacama Desert, my eyes surrendered, and I began to drift off. Suddenly, without warning, my nostrils caught a whiff of a strange but familiar scent.

My intellect took its time to process exactly where I recognized the scent from. It was a distinctive smell, a smell I smelled hundreds of times before but there was a peculiar note about it this time.

Unexpectedly, the answer struck my thoughts. *It's Blue Magic!*

Every Sunday evening, in preparation for the school week ahead, G-Ma washed Roni's hair. Then, after the blow-drying phase, she moisturized her scalp with a blue hair grease called Blue Magic. There were different colors, like white and green, but G-Ma was partial to the blue. I've even used my fair share of the same hair grease to style my hair plenty of times.

I smelled that grease every weekend for the past year or so. Yet there was something foreign about it this time. It smelled scorched.

I had no clue what to do next. I wanted to open my eyes, but they felt as if they were glued shut. Terrified, I did the only thing I knew to do.

"Netra, you sleep?" I called out to my little sister who was the same age as Roni. Somehow, I knew she wasn't.

"No."

"Can you smell that?"

"Smell what?"

I sound like a square.

"You can't smell that burnt smell?"

"Nope," she responded irritatedly.

My friends were fast asleep so there was no option to validate with them what I already knew to be true.

I needed a plan, and I needed it fast.

Pull the blanket over your head.

After pulling the blanket over my head, I decided to open my eyes.

For a few seconds, I lay under the blanket, eyes wide open, lost in pure darkness. The essence of Blue Magic and smoke lingered in the air. The heat from my labored breathing filled the emptiness between my nose and the blanket.

Something inside nudged me to take a chance, so I did.

Slowly, I pulled the blanket from over my eyes, and they began to gaze over the room.

All of a sudden, there she was, plaits and all. It was her faceless silhouette, but without question, it was her.

Instantly, I felt my breath steady and a calm wash over me.

Tears fell from the outer canthus of one eye, and I heard a small voice utter,

"I'm okay."

Then, just like that, she was gone.

The Follow Through

During my next visit to my favorite spiritual shop, I ripped off the Bandaid.

"I'll take these and I'd like to sign up for the next psychic class," I affirmed as I placed the various selections of crystals I gathered for purchase on the glass counter.

"Which one would you like to sign up for dear?"

Well damn, how many are there?

"We have one on Monday at 6 p.m. taught by Steven and the other taught by Jules on Wednesday at 4 p.m. They're both great teachers," the shop owner Amelia confirmed in her thick English accent that always made my spirit giggle a touch every time I heard it.

Why not just do both?

"I'll do both!"

Did that just come out of my mouth?

My next order of business was to begin my death doula certification class that I enrolled in months before my reading.

Yes, there is such a thing as a death doula! Crazy right?!

I was first made aware of what a death doula was during my time as a hospice nurse and I must say, the work of a death doula sounded way more gratifying than that of a hospice nurse.

Through my death doula training, I was informed of a specific training called Spiritual Death Work: Near Death Experiences, Ancestral Veneration, Death Deities, and Psychopomps. It was a class that spoke to understanding how death is looked at through many different lenses and cultural perspectives.

Don't get me wrong, in our culture we're taught at a young age to honor our ancestors but I'd never known it to have a name or it to go as in-depth as it does.

By the end of this class, my mind was blown. Not only did I learn so much more about death and how it's celebrated around the world, I figured out a way to lean on Mother Mary, to learn more about who she was, and to hear the voices of Papa, G-Ma, and maybe even Roni for myself.

It's been a few years since I first signed up for those psychic mediumship classes, and although I now have my practice, I continue to take them to this day.

THE TOOL

What is ancestral veneration exactly?

If you look up the words ancestral veneration in the Merriam-Webster dictionary, you'll find absolutely nothing. Weird right?

However, you will discover the definition for ancestor worship is defined as "the custom of venerating deceased ancestors who are considered still part of the family and whose spirits are believed to have the power to intervene in the affairs of the living."

Now, this is somewhat close to what many cultures identify as ancestral veneration but it doesn't explain it in its entirety.

In many cultures, including mine of the African Diaspora, ancestral veneration is about the celebration of your ancestors, known and unknown, familial and non-familial. It's about honoring those who came before you and blazed the trail of your existence through practices such as ritual and reflection and keeping the lines of communication open to receive their guidance and wisdom. It's the belief of many religions and cultures around the world that the ancestors are closer to the Creator, the Divine, God, the Source, or whomever they identify as their higher power, if any at all. We remember, honor, and celebrate our ancestors here on Earth to display our gratitude for the protection, abundance, prosperity, and guidance that they provide us with every day.

Benefits of Ancestral Veneration

The practice of ancestor work offers a variety of benefits that include:

- Identifying and healing generational traumas and curses.
- Finding forgiveness or acceptance.
- The opportunity to understand and preserve your family lineage.
- Building a strong sense of connection.
- Enhancing your personal growth and self-understanding.
- Understanding of your ancestors' guidance and wisdom.

In moments of fear and distress, ancestral veneration provides me with the ability to stand firm and empowered. It's a daily reminder that despite the challenges along the way, I journey boldly with the resilience, strength, and wisdom of my ancestors guiding my footsteps.

Ancestral Veneration Practices

As you can imagine, the list of ways to honor our loved ones who have passed away is as long as my arm, but try not to let this overwhelm you. Although I will discuss a few ways that I honor my ancestors, don't get so caught up in practicing the way that I do or doing it just right. I encourage you to think outside the box by making it your own and rest assured your ancestors will be that much more appreciative and accepting of your authenticity.

Ways I Honor My Ancestors:

Creating an altar

What was once my vanity later became my ancestors' altar. This was my way of memorializing my loved ones. Nothing fancy, just a few pictures of Papa, G-Ma, and Roni, one or two heirlooms for each, a candle, and an incense holder. This became my sacred space, the space where I would pray to them about any and everything. No one was allowed to touch anything in our space.

Daily conversations

I began a habit of talking to my ancestors at the same time every day, once first thing in the morning as soon as my eyes opened and again a few moments before I closed them at night. I was very intentional about these times because it allowed me to be aware of the signs and synchronicities they sent throughout the day and in my dreams.

Voyage to my homeland

My partner and I both journeyed to our homeland of Africa to rediscover and learn more about our heritage. We visited the slave castles of the Ivory Coast, small villages where the highly respected mothers performed our naming ceremony, and stood barefoot in the river where our ancestors took their last baths before ultimately being transported by ships to their demise. This allowed me to establish an undeniable connection to my ancestors that I had not felt in my entire life.

Family recipes

Food is a love language in my family and many families in African culture. I inherited all of G-Ma and Papas' recipes from my mother and her sisters and practiced them until they were committed to memory. Although my diet has changed drastically, I still honor my ancestors by cooking and baking with their cherished recipes during holidays, Sunday dinners, family celebrations, and potlucks.

Other known practices:

- Keeping familial records, archives, and photos.
- Offerings of tobacco, spirit money, food, or wine are left at the altar or the grave site.
- Balloon releases on their date of birth or death.
- Prayers on the anniversary of their death.
- Candle lighting on the anniversary of their death.
- Gravesite maintenance and decorating.
- Family reunions/gatherings.

Venerating Your Ancestors For Guidance

Trust me, this isn't as complicated as your human mind is making it out to be, so take a soothing breath, be calm, and trust the process.

1. Just Talk

It's truly as simple as just talking! It doesn't have to be a formality, but for those who need a little structure, try this:

Grab an index card or any piece of paper and write out the names of the ancestors that you'd like to honor and celebrate. Now recite these words:

"Ancestors, known and unknown, (then state the names of your ancestors you wrote on your paper out loud). I call upon you for your guidance and wisdom."

Now talk. Whether you speak to them for two minutes or twenty, speak from the heart. Speak about your challenges and successes, or ask for advice and guidance. Be sure to approach them as humble and true to you as can be. Always end your conversations with gratitude and thanks. Continue engaging in these conversations during the same time every day so that you and spirit develop a routine.

Be mindful of which ancestor you call on for guidance. Call on certain ancestors for specific needs. For instance, if you need guidance with increasing your abundance or prosperity, don't call on your great uncle Manny, who had a gambling addiction and lost everything because of it.

Now, let's take it a step further.

2. Sacred Space

Find a quiet area in your home that you can designate to just them, preferably out of sight from visitors if possible. Take the time to decorate and adorn this space however you see fit. Perhaps you remember me mentioning earlier that I turned the vanity in our walk-in closet into my sacred space and used pictures, heirlooms, candles, and incense to memorialize my ancestors. Personalize it how you like, but have fun with it. Make it as simplistic or elaborate as you want. During moments of distress, crisis, or delight, share it with them in your sacred space out loud or in your thoughts. Your sacred space is also the perfect place to have your daily conversations with your ancestors.

3. Listen

Be open to receiving guidance and answers from anywhere at any time. They may come from a song that randomly plays while you're in the lobby of your doctor's office or from a movie that you're watching on family night. Pay close attention to your dreams. I'd also advise you to keep a dream journal and write down all of your dreams (at least the ones you can remember). You'd be pleasantly surprised at how often our ancestors visit us in our dreams with messages.

Listening requires us to hear with our spiritual ears, not our outer ones, i.e., meditation. It invites us to abandon the limitations that we've placed on ourselves as human beings and tune out the worldly sounds that muffle the whispers of spirit. Prayer is where you go to ask for guidance; meditation is where you hear the answers.

Ancestral veneration honors the spirits of those who came before us, recognizing their continued presence and influence in our lives. Rooted in the belief that life extends beyond death, it celebrates the connection between the living and the departed. Many of us already practice ancestral veneration without realizing it through family traditions, sharing stories about loved ones, or keeping heirlooms that hold their memory. Lighting a candle in remembrance, saying their names out loud, or seeking their wisdom in times of need are subtle acts of reverence. By recognizing these daily practices, we deepen our connection to our ancestors, keeping their legacy alive.

We don't worship dead people; we pay homage to our ancestors and understand that they live within our DNA. They are the closest thing we have to the spiritual realm

~African Proverb

LèVonta White, LPN, CD(DONA), EOLD, RMT, Light Worker is the CEO and founder of Lighthouse Effect, where she provides professional support for those going through a major life event or change. It's her mission to be a guiding light on their journey to wellness, no matter the destination.

After being a nurse in the medical profession for 15 years, LèVonta decided to take a more holistic approach to life, death, and all everything in between. Her passion for life's most pivotal moments inspired her to become a certified birth doula, offering support and guidance to families during childbirth. She later became a certified death doula, providing comfort and dignity to individuals and families during the end-of-life process.

As a Reiki Master Teacher, LèVonta promotes healing and balance through energy work, helping clients achieve emotional and spiritual well-being. Her intuitive gifts as a psychic medium allow her to offer meaningful connections and messages of clarity, closure, and hope from loved ones who have passed.

She creates transformative and healing experiences for her clients through her unique blend of expertise and compassion.

When it's "me time," LèVonta enjoys herbalism, reading, cuddling with her partner, and game nights with her family. She also shares a beloved passion for sacred solitude and content creation.

Connect with LèVonta:

Website: https://www.lighthouseeffectllc.com
Youtube: https://www.youtube.com/@TheLighthouseEffectHealing
Facebook: https://www.facebook.com/profile.php?id=100084346817026
Instagram: https://www.instagram.com/mrslevontawhite

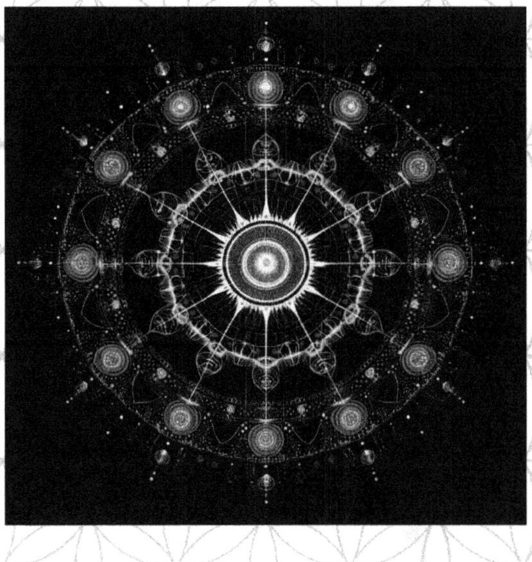

CHAPTER 12

ELEVATE THE RELATIONSHIP

Build Emotional Connection and Trust

By Kiela Kasomany

MY STORY

There are points in our lives that will help make us or break us. Then there are points which do both. This is my journey from chaos to clarity.

I was sitting alone on a cold bench. I just stared out the window from the hospital. I wanted to be by myself, away from people. I wanted to scream out loud. Internally I was.

I don't want to be here! Why? Why?

The city of Boston was illuminated so brightly by the sun that it almost hurt my eyes. I had been crying so much that my eyes felt completely raw.

My partner Will was undergoing surgery for his third valve replacement. Will's family and I waited with a growing sense of apprehension as the operation went over by hours. Will had been born with aortic stenosis. He had surgery to replace a valve when he was a child. It was made clear that the new valve would eventually need to be replaced. As Will got older, it would start failing. And it did. Will had his second aortic valve replacement a few months ago. We all thought it was a successful surgery. How terribly wrong we were!

Will had been sick, and his doctor's office diagnosed him with the flu. It wasn't the flu. It was much more serious! Will had an infection in his newly replaced aortic valve. He needed to have another heart surgery to replace it. I was cautiously optimistic.

Ok, he's only 33years old and physically fit. I know he will be fine after the surgery. He'll recover and we will go back to building our life together with Thaila and Malia.

When the surgeon came out, my optimism tanked. He didn't have a smile on his face. His eyes looked tired and almost sorrowful. The surgeon explained to us, "The valve is so badly infected I could almost just pluck it out of the heart. I replaced the valve, but Will is now battling infection, and it's rapidly spreading."

As I sat there on the bench, I cried out silently to God. God was my last resort. I tried to bargain with God, too. I grew up with a father who believed in nothing and a mother who believed in too much. I never had to really consider my beliefs until now. Is there even really a God?

God, please, I will do anything. I will commit to serving you. I promise to be a better person. I will raise my girls up to be the best that they can be and help them to make this world better for everyone they come in contact with. Please just bring Will back to us! Please, please!

God either didn't hear me or chose to ignore me because the next day, we were given even worse news. "Will's organs are beginning to shut down, and his body is going into septic shock. If, by chance, a miracle happens and he gets through this, he'll most likely end up in a wheelchair with possible brain damage. Some of his extremities may have to be amputated as well," the doctor explained.

I was in disbelief. *This can't be happening! Oh my God!*

Another couple of days later, they brought us together in a meeting and told us we would have to decide when to withdraw life support.

How can we decide? Why can't we wait? What about miracles?

The doctors made it very clear, "Will is not going to recover from this."

There would be no miracle for our family. We were devastated.

I sat on a chair by Will's hospital bed and gently put my hand over his. His hand felt very swollen. I honestly couldn't think. And then hot tears poured down my face. I finally found my voice and began to speak to him.

"You can go. I will be okay. You just have to be there to watch our girls. Just promise to watch over our girls. I love you," I whispered to him.

My head felt heavy, and the pain in my chest made me all too aware of what a broken heart felt like. My heart mostly ached for my young daughters, who would never know their father's love. The girls were his whole world. His pride, his joy. The loss of that love for them is the one thing that, to this very day, still breaks me.

On January 9, 2011, Will gave us one final gift—the gift of not having to feel the guilt of pulling someone you love off life support. He passed away on his own terms. I was now a widow with a three-month-old baby and a two-and-a-half-year-old to raise by myself.

WHO AM I NOW?

After Will passed, something happened to me. I shifted. It was so slow at that time I didn't notice. I went through a lot of emotions. Anger, sadness, fear, you name it, I felt it. I hid my grief and sadness from my girls. I wanted to give them a stable life. To do that, I needed to start working on myself. I couldn't afford to be an emotional wreck. I found a self-help book and started with that. After I finished it, I bought another one and another. Grief shattered me, and I had to find a way to put myself back together. I put up a mirror and faced all the ugly things within myself. I started peeling away the layers. And like an onion, the more I peeled, the more I cried. There was trauma from being a child who grew up witnessing domestic violence. There were self-worth issues because I looked different and came from a different culture. Then there was the shame of a mental crisis when I was a teenager. I realized the most important relationship I had to heal and elevate was with myself.

Looking back, I believe it was the grieving process that began to open up my psychic awareness. I also think being very sick with the flu for two weeks ignited it some more. That was the first time I had the flu. My whole body was racked in agonizing pain. My mother insisted on coming to my house to take care of me. Her brilliant idea of care, however, was to shake me awake every thirty minutes or so. She was terrified I wouldn't wake up. She had this belief that if I went to sleep, I would die! She's a very superstitious Laotian woman, and there was no point in arguing with her. As soon as I was about to doze off, here was my lunatic mother shaking me awake. She kept me constantly in this sort of state where I was exhausted and sleep-deprived.

"Wake up, wake up! It's not good to sleep!" My mother would yell. Then, she left when she felt I was roused up enough.

I am in so much pain. Oh my God, my head hurts so much. I think I am going to die.

Hahaha. No you're not!

I heard the laughter and the voice in my head. But it didn't sound like me.

Oh great, I'm hearing voices. So I am going crazy, too!

No, you're not.

Okay, well that definitely was not me answering myself.

My mother's well-meaning care opened up a door I didn't know existed. For a while, I seriously doubted I could possibly be a medium. At first, I thought it was my mind playing tricks on me, but as time passed, I realized there was more to it. I tuned into an entirely different frequency. It took some time but I eventually learned to trust there was a connection happening.

BLENDING TWO WORLDS

In my career as a medical aesthetician, I initially tried to keep the mediumship/ spiritual aspect out of my work. It wasn't an easy journey to open up and share my abilities. For one thing, I didn't want our clients and patients to think I was crazy as I aimed a laser directly at their faces. I was very reluctant to let anyone know. Dr. Lach, the plastic surgeon I work with, was aware I was training and being mentored in mediumship. He encouraged it and helped me to see that my work as a medical aesthetician and medium were interconnected. Whether it's a scar on the surface or a wound in the heart, both are about healing. With his support, I learned to embrace these two very different sides of myself.

I no longer freak out if clients and patients find out about my mediumship. I did at first when Diane, our receptionist, somehow found my mediumship business cards and put them out for all to see. I tried to hide them, but she has a serious knack for finding things. She just placed them back again on the front counter. Eventually, I just gave up and let Diane win that battle. But by losing that battle, I gained the freedom to share who I was.

I never would've imagined my career, which on the surface seems almost superficial, could be so much more! My clients often opened up to me during appointments. They shared with me their fears, joys, and deepest secrets. Each and every one of them has a very unique story to tell. By listening and sharing in their pain, triumphs, and worries, a genuine connection of trust was built. Through the years I'm very grateful their trust in me turned to loyalty. Some of my clients have been coming to me for so long that our relationship began to evolve into one of deep friendship.

These connections we have to each other are what gives our life meaning. Finding that relationship and connection to my own self, to my own spirit was the first crucial step for me. That's where all connections start and end. It's what has allowed me to share myself fully and build the bridges for other relationships to grow and thrive. These next few steps help me to be supportive of the light of others while also being the brightest light I can be.

THE TOOL

Elevate The Relationship: Three Steps to Bring in More Love and Compassion

STEP 1: Morning Gratitude

This first step can be done at any time but I love doing it just upon opening my eyes in the morning. Your heart and mind won't have a chance to be inundated by any stress that may come during the day. Some mornings, my gratitude prayer is short and simple. Sometimes, it's more elaborate. Doing it first thing in the morning starts you off with a positive outlook and a high vibrational imprint throughout your day. There are so many things you can be grateful for. Just waking up is one of them! This is one of my short versions.

Thank you, God, for all that I have and all that you have given to me. Thank you for the many blessings in my life. Thank you, especially for my family and my friends, those that are here on Earth, and those that are here in spirit. In this space and in this time, I am so very grateful for_____.

STEP 2: Spiritual Water Bath

To be able to connect to myself and others (physical and non-physical) with love, I like to ensure I'm the clearest me possible. It also gives me a chance to have an ahh…moment. This is how to go about doing that.

Fill up a bathtub with warm water and add one to two cups of salt. You can use Epsom salt, sea salt or Himalayan salt. Add a few drops of uplifting essential oils. I always have on hand lavender, myrrh, frankincense and sage. Now, set your intention with your words or your thoughts. The most important thing is the feelings behind them. That is what gives power to your intention. If you lack the time for a bath or don't have a tub, you can also do this in the shower. You can use a salt scrub and apply it to your entire body. Then, you would set your intention as you use the salt scrub and rinse it off. Here is a sample of what I say.

Dear God, my dear angels and guides, please bless this water that I am about to bathe in. Please allow it to cleanse my heart, my mind, my soul, my body, my aura, my chakras, my meridians, my light body, and my emotional body. If there are any negativities, any and all negative attachments, any and all that is not for my highest and best, please remove it and transmute it to that of light and love. I ask that the clearest and highest vibration of your light, your love, and your grace flow through my heart, my mind, my soul, my body, my aura, my chakras, my meridians, my light body, and my emotional body. Thank you, God!

STEP 3: Align to Love

This next exercise helps me boost and amplify my inner love for myself and others around me. I do it after the spiritual bath. I can almost feel a slight buzzing afterwards. Let me know if you do, too!

In this next step, you can grab a crystal. A rose quartz or plain quartz would work. If you don't have one, that's fine, too. You want to find a quiet place to sit where you won't be disturbed for a little bit. Next, hold the crystal to your heart and place your intention to deepen your connection to your inner spirit and to God. Once the intention is placed, you can keep the crystal in one hand or cupped in both hands.

Start closing your eyes and take in three to four slow, deep breaths. As you do so, imagine yourself sitting in the middle of a column of bright gold light that extends all the way to the heavens and all the way down through the earth. You're completely surrounded by this golden column of light. As you slowly draw the next breath, imagine pulling up the energy from the earth through your body to just above your head. Hold your breath briefly for a second there. On your exhale, feel yourself pushing that energy from above your head straight up the column to go up and out to the cosmos. With your very next breath in, start to slowly pull down the energy from the heavens through the top of your head and down your body towards your lower abdomen. Hold the breath again briefly for a second. Then, with your exhale, push the energy back down towards the Earth. Keep repeating this pushing and pulling of energy for a few minutes. By doing this you're making a conscious link between you and heaven and earth energy. With your next deep breath in, feel yourself pulling the energy in from both heaven and Earth at the same time into your body. Do this a few more times as well.

You can then take a few deep, regular breaths now. Now turn your attention to your heart space. See and feel that there is a bright spark of light there. This is your divine inner light. Your light shines and twinkles like the most beautiful diamond. The more aware you are of your own light, the more you can see it glowing and growing brighter in intensity. It starts filling out your chest. With every breath in and out, your light fills your entire body and starts radiating in every direction. Allow your inner light to grow even bigger and move out past your physical body. Feel it move past the room you are sitting in and out past your house. Imagine your light going way out into outer space. You can see the stars and the planets all around you.

At this moment, bring to mind something or someone you love. Feel your love for them. Really feel the warmth of this love. Feel their love for you as well. Breathe in and out the love that is all around you. Stay present in this vibration of love.

You can now see and feel an even greater and brighter, intensely radiant white light surrounding you and hugging your own light. Your light intensifies even more as you recognize this as the divine light of God. Feel yourself completely blending with pure, unconditional love. You can feel yourself just expanding more and more. Now, just sit and breathe in divine love and breathe out divine love. When you feel complete, say a prayer of thanks and draw the energy back into your beautiful heart space.

After reading my story, I hope you continue to trust in your own journey, listen to your heart, and honor your own spirit. And if you ever find yourself in my chair, whether for an aesthetic treatment or a psychic/mediumship session, know that I am here to remind you of the beauty and strength that you have had inside you all along!

With much love,

Kiela

Kiela Kasomany is a medical aesthetician/ laser technician at Boston Surgical Group with over 20 years of experience. She is also a psychic and medium at Still Intuition. Kiela is also part of the Soul Journey Sundays team.

Kiela is a dedicated wife and mother of three beautiful girls. She enjoys nurturing their passions and supporting their personal growth. She loves traveling internationally and exploring the world with her family. In her spare time, she likes to plant beautiful flowers around her house and work in her garden. She began having an interest in crystals and gemstones and learning about their unique properties. She loves collecting them. Kiela is passionate about her work. She keeps up with the latest trends and technology in medical aesthetics by regularly attending seminars. She places great emphasis on growing and evolving in her psychic and mediumship development by continuing her studies and mentorships. She has an interest in Qigong, Feng Shui and Budgies.

Connect with Kiela:

Websites: https://stillintuition.com
              https://souljourneysundays.com

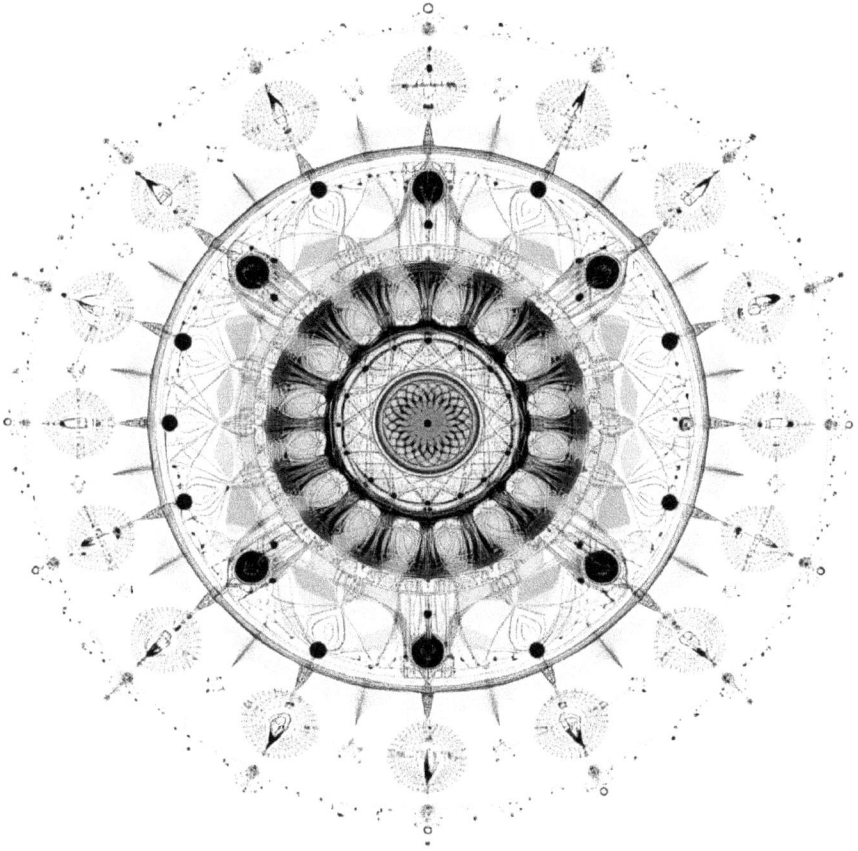

CHAPTER 13

STANDING HAPPILY ON YOUR OWN LIFE STAGE

Finding Your True Purpose and Step Into It

By Carm OSullivan, Spiritual Professor, Medium, Psychic, CHTP

MY STORY

Was this real? Was this a dream? Or was this a vision for the future?

I was on a stage in front of an audience of hundreds of people. They were all waiting. . .for me. I took a step onto center-stage with confidence, bursting with joy. No fear, no stage fright. It was a pivotal moment for me, a moment of being my truest self. I looked out into the audience and knew this was where I was meant to be. I can still envision it and feel it today.

I introduced myself.

"Hi everyone, my name is Carm OSullivan, and I'm here to demonstrate mediumship. More importantly though, I will be bringing messages of healing and loving connection to you from loved ones who have passed."

When I awoke from this vision (no, it wasn't a dream, nor was it real) I understood: This was my soul's purpose. I was asked to embrace the gifts I had been given as a medium. The very next day, I stepped out of the closet and started telling people who I really was. I changed my business cards to *Medium, Healer, and Psychic* and have done thousands of readings since. I've also done many large audience readings and I feel my best work is on the stage.

125

This vision was my *aha* moment, a kick in the pants from my guides to truly make me aware of who I was. I *had* to conquer my fear of being judged and not accepted and just trust. I let go of fear, knowing my angels and guides had my back, and my business has thrived ever since.

My back story is quite an energetic ride. I lived an interesting life with a brilliant bipolar schizoid mother and a father who spoke in tongues at his Catholic Pentecostal services. My mother was beautiful in appearance, graduated Summa Cum Laden, and spoke five languages. But, she was hospitalized many times because of her mental breakdowns. (Or so the doctors thought. I have come to believe she had psychic ability and was haunted by spirits who talked to her.) My father was a soft, loving soul, a kind, wise man who was a stutterer. His faith gave him strength to be with my mother until the end of their lives. Their gifts of connection were passed down to me.

Many nights as a child I quaked in fear in my bed because I felt people poking me. I knew spirits wanted to talk to me—and I was definitely not open to it. As I matured, lights turned on and off unexpectedly wherever I lived. Once I heard a voice come out of the speaker and tell me to, "get out." This event made me run outside my apartment unit feeling completely freaked out. *OH my god, I thought maybe I am crazy like my mom!*

I was always psychic and thought it was something everyone experienced. I was compelled to share random things to friends and family about their lives and also about their health or upcoming circumstances. Periodically, people circled back to me and validated what I shared. I had many people in my life tell me, "You're a healer." I heard this over and over for many years.

One day my decorator gave me a book on healing. *That's odd*, I thought. The book sat untouched for years. Then I got certified for Healing Touch Therapy and that book became my go-to source. Years later, I ran into the decorator and I asked why she'd given me the book. "I knew you would be using it in the future," she said. "I was told to give it to you by my guides."

I discounted all these messages but never forgot them. When I finally awakened, it all made sense. I like to call these messages my "aha moments," but my soul was not fully awake and not fully tuned into my higher self yet. So these taps on my shoulder were ignored or buried for future reference.

What's an "aha moment?" These are rare moments in life when you have an experience that gives you clarity or enlightenment about your life path and the direction your life should take. I like to call them "whispers from the soul," bringing clarity to your soul walk. Your higher self is providing you with a vision, a "God wink" moment, or a bonk on your head to help you see the clear path. For example, Dorothy from *The Wizard of Oz* was shown her path by Glinda (her guide) and told to follow the yellow brick road. When we are connected, our guides, angels, and higher self, we're given hints, taps, and more. The soul's higher self is your most profound intuitive guide, intimately aware of your life's destinies and the paths you're meant to walk. When I conduct a reading, I connect to your higher self to receive messages and insights that can help you move forward with clarity and purpose. In the classes I teach, my special hands-on exercises evoke the clarity of your gifts of intuition.

It's fascinating how often this resonates with my clients. I might say, "Have you considered this for your path?" And more often than not, they'll respond, "I was just thinking about that yesterday!" or "My friend just mentioned that too!" These repetitions are not coincidences; they are signals from your higher self urging you to pay attention. If you hear something more than once, it's time to start considering that path seriously.

These illuminating moments are often gentle nudges, guiding you toward something you've been hesitating to pursue. But what's holding you back from stepping forward? For me, stepping into my role as a medium was deeply intimidating. I knew skepticism could shape how others perceived me, and I was told countless times that this work was "evil" or "of the devil." In the past, I tried to change the minds of those driven by fear, but I no longer feel the need to convince anyone otherwise. I know my gift comes from God, and it is my true purpose. In pursuing my gifts, I lost a few friends and had to justify and explain my newfound passion. Yet, at the same time, I discovered many people leaning in—curious and open to learning more about death, our souls, and the connections that transcend this life.

Fear is often the biggest obstacle, blocking us from stepping onto your stage. But ask yourself: *What is my fear really based on?* Is it financial concerns, self-doubt, fear of judgment, or the possibility of failure? Is it your ego trying to hold you back, keeping you safely within your comfort zone?

The key to overcoming fear is through awareness. These moments of guidance from your higher self are like gentle taps on the shoulder, softly whispering: *This is for you. It's time to act.* If you're not paying attention, you might miss them. Recognizing these signs requires mindfulness and trust in the process. Once you know your path, ask yourself what fears are stopping you from pursuing this new life goal. For me it was about caring less about what other people thought of me and allowing my joy of the work to propel me forward.

How do you know you are truly aligned with your soul path at this very moment?

In life, you'll be led down many different roads, each contributing to your soul's journey and ultimate destination. Not every job or passion will feel like your "soul job," but each experience adds depth and understanding to your life.

From an early age, our paths are shaped by opportunities that teach us valuable lessons. For example, your first job as a teenager might've been something simple, like working at a burger joint. I worked at Burger King and loved it. Later, I moved on to roles as a store marketing agent, decorator, and even the top shoe salesperson at JC Penney.

Looking back, those jobs were more than just work—they were lessons. They taught me confidence and how to connect with people on a deeper level. I learned to read people's energy and understand what draws them into a place, whether it was a store, a product, or even an idea. These experiences were all stepping stones, preparing me for the work I do now, where connection and intuition are at the heart of everything.

Each road, no matter how unrelated it may seem at the time, is part of a greater plan, helping you build the skills and wisdom you'll carry forward into your true calling.

Some people know from an early age what they hope to be in life. Some figure it out slowly as they grow and receive more life experience. As a child, I played "school" with my dolls and I was the teacher. It was embedded in me from early on. I pursued a teaching degree in college at Cal State Northridge but never formally used that degree until I moved into my spiritual being at 52 years old. It's interesting when you reflect on your life, the tidbits you receive along the way will be aligned to your soul work. Below is my method of connection.

THE TOOL

Finding Your Life Stage: A Journey to Self-Discovery Exercise

Everyone has a stage to stand on in life. My calling is mediumship and spiritual teaching—connecting others to their loved ones and educating people about connection and energy. A stage is not just a platform for passion or career; it is a pivotal moment of alignment with your true purpose.

When you step onto your stage, are you smiling and confident, feeling grounded and centered in your heart? To discover your stage, you must reflect on your past and present using tools such as breathwork, meditation, and quiet introspection. This guide will help you reconnect with your higher self and uncover the stage you are meant to stand on today.

Step 1: Gather Your Tools

- Notebook or journal: Choose something special to hold your thoughts and reflections.
- Pencil, pen, and eraser: Use the eraser to release judgment of your work; erase and rewrite freely.
- Childhood picture or memory: Bring your favorite childhood picture to use in this exercise. If you don't have one, simply bring along a cherished memory of your childhood self. This will help you connect with your inner child and guide your reflections.

Step 2: Setting the Stage for the Process of Connection

- Choose a clutter-free, serene space.
- Sit in a comfortable chair or cushion.
- Surround yourself with items that bring you peace or joy (e.g., a candle, plants, or meaningful objects). This creates a peaceful environment that allows your soul to relax.

Step 3: Decide on Sound

What atmosphere helps you feel centered and grounded? • Quiet: Sit in silence to hear your inner voice clearly.

- Music: Choose high-vibrational, soft spiritual music (easily found on YouTube, Spotify or similar platforms).
- White Noise playing in the background will help block outside exterior noise.

Step 4: Set Your Intention

Write a clear intention in your notebook. For example:

- Show me the path for my highest journey.
- Show me the stage of life I need to be standing on.
- Begin with a prayer, an intention, and or by calling in your guides or angels to support you.

Step 5: Center Yourself with Breathwork

Practice the 4-7-8 breathing technique to calm your body and open your mind:

1. Breathe in through your nose for four counts.
2. Hold your breath for seven counts.
3. Exhale through your mouth for eight counts.
   Repeat until you feel relaxed and open to receiving insight.

Step 6: Ask Yourself the Big Question

- *Am I already standing on my stage?*
- If yes, describe your stage in detail.
- If no, begin listing the things that make you happy and bring you joy.
- Example: I love the outdoors. I love helping others. *I love being creative. I love to garden. I am most happy teaching others.*

Step 7: Reconnect with Your Younger Self

- Ask your younger self: What did you want to be when you grew up? You choose the age. I suggest anywhere from an early memory to 18 years of age.
- Look at a childhood picture: If you have a childhood picture, take a moment to look at it closely. What do you see in your younger self's eyes? Is there curiosity, joy, or determination?
- No picture? No problem: If you don't have a picture, think back to a beautiful memory or moment from that time in your life. Let the feelings and imagery of that memory guide you.
- Write it down: Record your answer and how it felt to declare your dream as a child or teenager.
   This step helps you reconnect with your purest aspirations and uncover the seeds of your true purpose.

Step 8: Reflect on Feedback from Others

- Consider feedback: Has anyone ever told you what they think you're good at or where your strengths lie? Reflect on these comments.
- Astrological insights: If you know your astrological natal birth chart, review it and consider any guidance or revelations it provides. For deeper insight, see a trusted astrologer.
- Aptitude tests: Did you ever take an aptitude test? What were the results, and how did they resonate with you?
- Write your reflections: Record all these insights in your notebook, including how each one made you feel at the time.

This step is about noticing patterns and external affirmations that might align with your inner knowledge.

Step 9: Identify Your "Aha Moments"

- Recall as many "aha moments" as you can—times when you knew you were on the right path.
- Ask yourself: Did I follow those moments? If not, why? • Write freely without judgment.

Step 10: Connect the Dots

Review your notes and reflect:

- Do you see recurring themes or patterns?
- Where do your heart and head align?
- Are you on a path that feels soul-worthy?

Step 11: Identify Your Fear or Fears

Step 1: Write down what's holding you back—financial concerns, judgment, failure, or self-doubt. Be honest.

Step 2: Understand its source

Ask yourself:

- Where does this fear come from?
- Is it based on past experiences, societal pressure, or my own insecurities?

- Is this fear-based or connected to a limited belief?

Step 3: Reframe your fear

Challenge your fear by flipping it into a positive statement:

- "What if I fail?" becomes "What if I succeed?"
- "People will judge me" becomes "The right people will support me."

Step 4: Listen to your higher self

Take deep breaths, quiet your mind, and ask:

- What is my next step?
- How can I move forward with courage?
- Visualize walking forward embracing the fear with a smile!

Step 5: Take one small action

Choose a small step—research, a conversation, or setting an intention. Taking action builds confidence.

Step 12: Write down your conclusions

- *Have I listened to my soul, my child-self, and my higher self's "aha moments"? Have I faced and addressed my fears?*

Closing Reflection

This exercise can be completed all at once or broken down into daily steps. Whichever approach you choose, be sure to keep detailed notes each time you enter a state of connection.

Remember, this is just the beginning of creating your life stage. It's a journey of reflection, self-understanding, and deepening your connection with your truer self. By listening to your inner voice and trusting the guidance of your higher self, you can step confidently onto your stage and align with your soul's purpose.

Ready to go deeper?

I guide others in finding their life path through reflection, Human Design, Astrological insights and connection to their higher self. Go to my website to set up an appointment to explore this further! I also offer classes in many soul subjects.

Carm OSullivan, Heart to Heart Medium and The Spiritual Professor

Carm O'Sullivan is a compassionate healer, Medium, Psychic and spiritual teacher who embraces all faiths and beliefs. Her journey into healing began in 2012, learning to specialize in Reiki and Healing Touch Therapy. Through these practices, she mastered the art of using energy work to reduce anxiety, alleviate pain, and enhance overall well-being.

Carm's intuitive gifts as an evidential medium and psychic have flourished alongside her healing practice. She has trained with renowned mentors such as John Holland and Janet Nohavec and is currently under the guidance of Spirit Artist and Pastor of The Journey Within Church, Joe Shiel. This mentorship has refined her ability to create spirit portraits during readings, capturing the essence of loved ones in spirit and bringing comfort and validation to those grieving.

As a psychic, Carm connects with clients' higher selves to identify challenges and offer guidance, empowering them to move toward more peaceful and fulfilling lives. Her readings include Human Design and Astrological insight. She encourages self-reflection and provides awareness into overcoming personal obstacles with compassion and clarity.

With over 15 years of experience as an educator and holding a degree in education from California State Northridge, Carm provides mentorship in intuitive development and mediumship with "in person" and online courses. She also leads mediumship and intuitive practice circles and hosts a podcast called Getting to the Heart of the Matter.

Carm loves her work and deeply values the clients and students who are brought to her. Visit her website to learn about upcoming classes and or to schedule an insightful session.

Connect with Carm:

Website: http://carmosullivan.com
Facebook: http://www.facebook.com/carmelo'sullivan
Instagram: https://www.instagram.com/carmosullivan
Youtube: youtube.com/@carmelosullivan5405
TikTok: https://www.tiktok.com/@carmosullivan

"In every walk with nature, one receives far more than he seeks."

~ **John Muir**

CHAPTER 14

THE HEALING POWER OF NATURE

The Path to Awaken Your True Self

By Michele Cutler, MMP

MY STORY

My connection to nature didn't arrive with fanfare and epiphanies—it crept in quietly, like a forgotten melody, until I could no longer ignore its call to something deeper within me.

My Love of Nature

Growing up in Southern California, one might envision a life steeped in the hustle of an urban city, but my experience was quite different. I grew up in an era when the sprawling Los Angeles area still bore the charm of untouched landscapes, horse farms, and fragrant orange groves. As development began encroaching on these cherished staples, my family relocated to the tranquil outskirts, where nature was still more than a whisper.

Surrounded by the striking beauty of rolling hills, giant oak trees, and the melodic sounds of chirping birds, I found tranquility in a world that felt alive and sacred. I often took these wild wonders for granted in my youthful innocence, unaware of their profound impact on my spirit. It wasn't until I encountered the stark absence of the untouched world that I fully grasped the uniqueness and significance of the natural landscape of my childhood.

I was immersed in the wilderness, with experiences that unfolded unpretentiously around me. The Girl Scout outings were particularly memorable; we enjoyed evenings huddled around crackling campfires, the air filled with the warmth of glowing flames, and the excitement of sharing ghost stories that sent shivers down our spines, comforted by the familiar scent of overcooked marshmallows. My family often embarked on joyful adventures aboard our ski boat, gliding across shimmering waters or camping beside serene lakes where we cast our lines, hoping to reel in the day's catch. The beauty of nature was ever-present, and I never felt the urge to seek it out beyond what was readily available.

As an adult, it became clear that my heart was still drawn to the great outdoors, even if I wasn't fully aware. I taught snow skiing in the stunning Sierra Nevada Mountains, where the crisp air sometimes took my breath away. I also visited horse ranches and connected deeply with these magnificent creatures while assisting an equine veterinarian. The rhythm of life outside fueled my soul, and my career choices mirrored my enduring passion for the natural world.

Surprisingly, I chose a career that whisked me across the country in a silver tube as a flight attendant for a major airline. Despite my best efforts, the monotony of shuttling between sterile hotel rooms, bustling airport terminals, and cramped airplanes gradually drained the pleasure from my adventures. Sometimes even waking up in the middle of the night and wondering, *Where am I?* The days and years began to blur into a dizzying series of flights and hurried meals, with fewer opportunities to feel the sun on my face.

On my precious days off, I gravitated toward open spaces, seeking refuge in the calm of the natural world. After my riding lessons, I often spent all day at the barn, breathing in the earthy scents of hay and the horses providing a comforting soundtrack. I felt renewed solace, soaking up the sun and feeling the dirt beneath my boots. The connection to nature rejuvenated my spirit, reminding me of simpler delights beyond the silver tube. Whether grooming a horse or appreciating the quiet, I reconnected with myself and the rhythms of life I longed for while hopping time zones and flying over oceans.

This wasn't merely a fondness for being outside; it was a vital lifeline. Nature was so much more than just something I enjoyed; it was an essential component of my well-being, though I struggled to recognize its true impact at the time.

I immersed myself in studying natural resources and conservation biology, earning my degree driven by a deep passion for understanding and protecting the environment. My adventures took me across breathtaking landscapes in various stunning countries. I hiked, rode horses, and explored lush forests, serene mountains, and picturesque countrysides. Each journey soothed my soul and connected me to something bigger than myself.

I also devoted my time to volunteering with various conservation and environmental education organizations, passionately raising awareness and embodying the values behind the saying, *"What we value, we tend to protect."* These interconnected experiences helped me understand my strong bond with the outdoors, even if I didn't completely realize it then.

What about nature drew me in so profoundly? I often found myself pondering the roots of this deep-seated passion. *Why am I always inspired to spend countless vacations and adventures in the heart of the natural world?* I often thought. Each experience felt like a thread intricately woven into the tapestry of my connection with the environment, sparking curiosity at every turn.

Following My Path

My journey to becoming a psychic/medium was, to say the least, unexpected. Throughout my life, I regarded my ability to "just know" as nothing more than an oddity, a quirky trait that set me apart from others. I didn't set out on an intentional journey to become a medium; rather, I believed mediumship was a rare and mystical gift, a treasure granted only to a fortunate few at birth. Only later, as I delved deeper into this fascinating realm, I understood this ability could be nurtured—much like any other inherent talent—through study, mentorship, and committed practice. This eye-opening revelation illuminated a path filled with exciting opportunities for discovery and personal growth, unveiling new horizons I never dared to imagine.

My career as a flight attendant opened the door to a fascinating exploration of my passion for the mystical realms. During my layovers in the UK, where one could find an abundance of psychic and mediumship classes, I sought out workshops and lessons, immersing myself in the teachings of talented tutors and seasoned mediums. Life up in the clouds can sometimes feel monotonous, with little room for advancement or personal growth. Many of my colleagues seek fulfillment beyond the confines of the cabin doors. In this search, I discovered my true calling—a journey into the esoteric that ignited my spirit and enriched my life.

With my newfound curiosity, I eagerly delved into the captivating world of mediumship and psychic abilities. It kindled a deep enthusiasm. I joined a vibrant development circle that quickly felt like a second family. I sought knowledgeable tutors whose wisdom illuminated my path and even traveled across the pond several times to the esteemed Arthur Findlay College. There, I honed my skills under the guidance of notable instructors and formed deep, lasting friendships with fellow students who shared my fervor for the mystical arts.

My journey in developing mediumship was a winding road characterized by periods of both growth and self-doubt. Interestingly, it reflected my adventures in nature, with steep hills to climb promising the reward of a beautiful waterfall. There were days when I considered giving up altogether, overwhelmed by feelings of inadequacy. I wrestled with nagging thoughts. *Perhaps I'm not good enough to be a medium, or People deserve a more skilled medium than me, and My peers surpassed me in talent.*—a pitfall I dubbed "comparisonitis."

Nonetheless, this journey forced me to confront my limiting beliefs and examine the barriers I unconsciously built around myself. It became clear that if I wanted to nurture my mediumship, I first had to heal the medium—me. This realization led me on a quest for self-healing, prompting the question: *How do I heal myself?*

Heal the Medium, Heal the Mediumship

While pursuing my degree, I was introduced to the theory regarding the strength and value of the connection between humans and nature. One of the foundational books on this topic is Richard Louv's *The Last Child in the Woods,* which I once co-taught in a book study to elementary school educators. Later, I discovered Florence Williams's book *The Nature Fix.* This uplifting work was transformative for me over time. Williams embarks on several scientific explorations to understand how nature benefits human beings. It turns out that nature possesses remarkable healing qualities. Various research studies have shown that immersing ourselves in the natural world offers numerous advantages, including relieving stress, reducing cortisol levels, improving blood pressure and heart rate, enhancing mood, and alleviating symptoms of anxiety and depression.

Several years ago, I conducted my own experiment due to high cortisol levels from frequent travel and jet lag, which affected my sleep. Over six months, I made a concerted effort to spend more time outdoors by taking walks in parks, starting a vegetable garden, and spending quality time with my pets. I noticed a significant improvement in my health, and at my next doctor's appointment, my physician observed a notable drop in my cortisol levels. "What have you been doing to convince your body that a tiger isn't chasing you?" my doctor asked. I replied, "The only thing I can attribute it to is spending more time in nature."

Experiences like this led me to ponder a more profound question: *if nature could mend the physical strains of my human existence, what healing might it offer to the very essence of my soul?*

Nature nurtured not just my physical body but my essence—the part of me that thrives on intuition, creativity, and the connections I share with the spirit world. It was a steadfast companion, always present, providing insights and comfort, much like the spirit world. Now, I weave this deep appreciation for nature into the fabric of my daily life. More importantly, I yearn to inspire others to embark on their own journeys of healing, encouraging them to embrace the transformative power of the great outdoors and to open themselves to the serenity and wisdom that nature generously offers.

Nature provides profound insights that can guide us on our personal journeys, especially during moments of confusion. For example, when I found a bat on my horse's stall door, I was reminded of its symbolism of strength and navigating darkness. Similarly, hawks often appear when I get caught up in details, urging me to see the bigger picture, while herons remind me to embrace patience and serenity. These animal encounters aren't mere coincidences; they serve as guiding lights, helping us find healing and clarity in tough times.

One of the most profound lessons I gleaned from observing the natural world is the importance of being attuned to its rhythms. Nature unfolds in an effortless cycle of seasons, each distinct and rich with meaning—winter, spring, summer, and fall. However, there are deeper intricacies within these cycles that often go unnoticed.

For example, as fall approaches, the vibrant greens of summer begin to fade, and the trees gracefully release their leaves. This seasonal shift teaches us an essential lesson about letting go; it reminds us to relinquish the burdens and attachments that no longer serve our growth.

If we can align ourselves with the wisdom rooted in the seasons, we can cultivate a greater sense of balance and harmony in our lives. We can learn to embrace the flow of change just as nature does. Each season offers a unique opportunity for reflection and growth, inviting us to evolve alongside it.

A few years ago, right after the New Year, I struggled to set goals, establish reasonable resolutions, and create personal and business plans. This time of year is usually exciting because it involves looking toward the future, but I felt off-balance, overwhelmed, and frustrated. My lack of motivation only added to my feelings of defeat.

One snowy morning, I lay on my yoga mat, gazing out the window at the snowflakes dancing through the air. Surrounded by multiple windows, I felt like I was inside a snow globe. The recurring thoughts of *New Year, new you. Why can't I get organized like everyone else?* swirled in my mind.

As I breathed deeply through the stillness, it dawned on me: *right now, all I want to do is hibernate.* Everything within me, along with the nature outside my window, was urging me to slow down, reflect, and embrace the tranquility of the season. I realized I was resisting the significance of this time of year. If I could honor what nature taught me and align myself with the natural world, I'd live more harmoniously.

One of the most profound things I've done is learn to balance with the seasons. This practice helped me connect my human side with my soul and allowed me to live more in harmony with the natural world. Not too many generations ago, our ancestors were more in tune with nature and its messages and lessons. So, why can't we strive to be aligned as well?

THE TOOL

Establishing Alignment and Balance with the Seasons

Nature is a free source of wonder for everyone. You don't need a long journey to connect with its beauty; sometimes, the simplest moments are the most enriching. Step outside to breathe in fresh air, admire the clouds, or listen to rustling trees. If you can't go outdoors, bring nature home with houseplants or a calming fountain. Visualization can also provide some of the same benefits as being in nature. If you're interested, visit my website for a guided visualization to connect with your sacred space in nature and a full version of working with the seasons. Click here: https://www.walkthepathwithin.com/intuitive-entrepreneur-book-extras

Nature operates in cycles and constantly transforms, much like our lives. Change is inevitable, and while it can create fear and uncertainty for some, it also offers exciting opportunities. Observing nature can teach us to embrace change and connect more deeply with our true selves.

Winter signifies introspection and inner reflection. It's a time for rest and renewal, allowing us to shed old layers and prepare for new growth. This season encourages exploration of our inner selves and confronting our shadows, teaching patience and resilience while emphasizing the importance of embracing stillness to hear our intuition.

Ways to Connect with Winter

1. *Embrace Rest and Stillness:* Set aside quiet reflection, meditation, or journaling time. And learn to say no! Allow yourself to rest and recharge without guilt.
2. *Practice Inner Reflection:* Explore your emotions, confront limiting beliefs, and focus on personal growth through shadow work or deep introspection through journaling or meditation.
3. *Create Cozy Rituals:* Light candles, enjoy warm teas, and create a nurturing space to encourage feelings of comfort and safety during darker, colder days.
4. *Set Intentions for Renewal:* Use the energy to reflect on what you want to release and the new beginnings you wish to cultivate in the coming year.
5. *Honor Nature's Dormancy:* Spend time observing the stillness of nature—bare trees, frosty mornings, or the silence of snowfall. Let it remind you of the power of quiet regeneration.

Spring symbolizes rebirth, renewal, and awakening. It marks a time of growth when nature flourishes. It offers new beginnings and endless possibilities, reminding us that transformation is possible after dark winters. Spring encourages us to plant seeds of intention, nurture our dreams, and embrace change, celebrating the beauty of renewal.

Ways to Connect with Spring

1. *Plant Seeds of Intention:* Write down your goals and dreams, symbolizing them by planting seeds or flowers to care for and nurture.
2. *Spend Time Outdoors:* Take walks in nature to witness the budding trees, blooming flowers, and awakening wildlife. Let the energy of growth inspire you.
3. *Embrace New Beginnings:* Start a new creative project, hobby, or practice or revive an old one that brings joy and renewal to your life.
4. *Declutter Your Space:* Engage in physical and emotional spring cleaning to make room for fresh energy and growth.
5. *Practice Gratitude:* Reflect on the opportunities and possibilities blooming in your life and express gratitude for the fresh starts spring offers.

Summer represents abundance, vitality, and fulfillment, marking a peak time of growth and expression in nature. It is a season of celebration and joy, reminding us to bask in the sunlight and appreciate our surroundings. Summer encourages living in the present, embracing life's blessings, and confidently pursuing our dreams while sharing our gifts with the world.

Ways to Connect with Summer

1. *Celebrate Abundance:* Reflect on and appreciate your progress and the fruits of your labor. Celebrate your wins, big and small.
2. *Spend Time with friends and family:* Enjoy time together outside, whether at the beach, a park, or your backyard, enjoying your favorite activities.
3. *Live in the Moment:* Focus on mindfulness and being fully present, savoring simple joys like picnics, gatherings, or summer nights under the stars.
4. *Express Your True Self:* Wear bright colors, pursue passions, or engage in activities that allow you to radiate your authenticity and confidence.
5. *Harvest Inspiration:* Use the peak of nature's growth as inspiration for your creative and spiritual endeavors.

Fall symbolizes harvest, transition, and letting go. It's a time for reflection as nature prepares for the colder months. This season encourages us to release old patterns and embrace change, highlighting the beauty of impermanence. Fall invites us to honor the cycles of life, find beauty in the changing leaves, and welcome the gifts of release and renewal.

Ways to Connect with Fall

1. *Release What No Longer Serves You:* Engage in rituals like journaling or burning old papers representing beliefs, patterns, or situations you're ready to let go of.
2. *Honor the Harvest:* Reflect on your achievements over the year and celebrate your growth and accomplishments.
3. *Practice Gratitude for Change:* Embrace transitions by appreciating the beauty in impermanence—watching the leaves fall, for example, as a symbol of natural change.
4. *Simplify and Prepare:* Use the season to declutter your life, simplify your commitments, and prepare for the slower pace of winter.
5. *Spend Time in Nature:* Take walks in the crisp autumn air, notice the changing colors of the leaves, and feel the grounding energy of the season.

Michele Cutler, MMP, is a medium, intuitive life coach, mentor, and spiritual teacher who is passionate about helping individuals connect with their soul selves through the wisdom of nature. As the founder of Walk the Path Within™, Michele combines a down-to-earth, pragmatic approach with a deep spiritual connection to offer a unique and holistic perspective on personal growth and spiritual development.

With extensive training in mediumship from renowned tutors in the UK and the US, including the prestigious Arthur Findlay College, and a degree in natural resources, interdisciplinary studies in conservation biology, and a Master's of Management Practice, Michele brings a wealth of experience and expertise that fosters a deep appreciation for the natural world.

Michele is dedicated to guiding clients to connect with their inner selves and find direction and clarity through nature-based practices and intuitive insights. By blending scientific knowledge with spiritual wisdom, Michele empowers individuals to live in harmony with themselves and the environment, fostering a deeper understanding of their soul's journey.

Whether through mediumship readings, personalized coaching, mentorship, or spiritual teaching, Michele's nurturing guidance and profound insights inspire clients to embark on a transformative journey of self-discovery and spiritual growth.

In her spare time, Michele enjoys the great outdoors, hiking scenic trails, and finding solace in quiet walks. An amateur genealogist, she loves uncovering her family's history and unique stories. The theater, especially musicals, is close to her heart for its storytelling and music. Michele eagerly explores new places, embracing different cultures and landscapes. Above all, she cherishes moments with her husband and their dogs, cats, and horses.

Connect with Michele:

Website: https://www.walkthepathwithin.com/
Facebook: https://www.facebook.com/walkthepathwithin
Instagram: https://www.instagram.com/walkthepathwithin/
YouTube: https://www.youtube.com/@WalkthePathWithin

"It's moments, not hours that will shift your business."

~ Deborah Drummond

CHAPTER 15

INTUITIVE SUCCESS

How to Build a Life by Following Your Intuition

By Deborah Drummond, Entrepreneur and Speaker

The path to aligning your life and work with intuition is a courageous journey of trust, transformation, and self-discovery. For those willing to take that leap, the rewards are life-changing. What follows is not just my story but also a guide to how intuition shaped my life and career. It's a reminder that listening to your inner voice can lead to extraordinary outcomes..

MY STORY

I remember the night that changed everything. It was around 4 a.m. I had just returned from work in the music world. After another evening at the club, my colleagues and I joined the band for dinner and drinks. It was a routine I followed countless times. But that night, as I stood in front of the mirror to remove my makeup, something inexplicable happened.

The mirror went black. My reflection disappeared. Panic surged through me as I stared at the void, unsure if it would return. When it did, I heard an unmistakable message: *You're done.*

Those two words carried a clarity I couldn't ignore. They weren't just about leaving my job—they signified the end of a chapter in my life. The next day, I called the club and resigned. It was an act completely out of character for me, and I had no plan for what would come next. Yet, that moment marked the beginning of a transformative journey.

145

This was over 25 years ago. That decision set me on a path of personal development and eventually led to my career in holistic well-being. The road was anything but straightforward. It was filled with coincidences, signs, and alliances that seemed almost magical. But it also demanded courage, especially as I ventured into a world still undiscovered and misunderstood by mainstream culture.

In those days, terms like "yoga," "chakras," and "aromatherapy" were foreign concepts to most people. There were no yoga studios on every corner, no gluten-free options, and certainly no mention of biohacking. Yet, somehow, I found myself stepping into this pioneering space.

As I reflect on that time, I realize how pivotal it was to trust my instincts. I had no guidebook or mentor in this new realm, and yet I felt a deep connection to the path unfolding before me. It wasn't just about exploring holistic practices— it was about discovering a way of life that resonated with my soul. Every step required faith, and every success reinforced my belief in the power of intuition.

FROM MUSIC TO MASSAGE

Transitioning from the high-energy music scene to the serene world of massage and holistic health was like moving from AC/DC to Enya. It felt like a complete identity shift. My first step into this new world came in the form of a simple flyer at a muffin shop. Something about it stood out to me, almost as if it called my name. It advertised a massage course, and despite knowing little about the field, I signed up.

The experience was transformative. As I worked on clients, I noticed my intuitive abilities growing stronger. At first, it was unsettling. I didn't understand what I was experiencing or how to articulate it. Then one day, a neighbor invited me to see a psychic. I was skeptical, but I went. The psychic's first words were, "Someone here is psychic and doesn't know what to do about it."

That moment was a turning point. It gave me permission to explore my abilities and use them as a guiding force in my career. Over time, I delved into massage, Ayurveda, aromatherapy, chakras, and intuitive services. Each modality deepened my understanding of the mind-body connection and helped me develop tools to support others on their journeys.

Looking back, I see how critical those early days were. The shift from music to massage wasn't just a career change — it was a reinvention of myself. It required me to shed old identities and embrace new possibilities. Each client I worked with became a teacher, revealing insights about the human spirit and the interconnectedness of all things. My intuition became my compass, guiding me through uncharted waters.

BUILDING A HOLISTIC CAREER

Over the years, I built a thriving career in holistic well-being. I worked with over 30,000 clients, founded a clinic, and hired a team of 18 staff members. I also created and formulated over 300 natural products and established two businesses distributing health products and gemstone jewelry across the country.

Each step was guided by intuition. One of the most rewarding aspects of this journey was witnessing the impact of my work on others. Clients shared stories of how a product or treatment transformed their lives. These moments reminded me why I started this journey—to bring healing and hope to those seeking it. Each success story fueled my passion and reaffirmed my commitment to following my intuition.

The path wasn't without challenges. Building a business from the ground up required resilience. There were days when self-doubt crept in, like *was this a good financial decision for my family* and I questioned my decisions. However, every time I leaned into my intuition, the answers became clear. It taught me to embrace uncertainty and view obstacles as opportunities for growth.

In hindsight, I realized intuition often provided solutions that logic couldn't. It acted as a bridge between my conscious goals and the deeper, often unseen forces guiding my journey. This connection became the foundation for not only my career but also my personal growth.

INTUITION IN PRACTICE

Explaining how intuition shaped my career would take volumes. But one thing is clear: intuition grows when nurtured. It requires bravery to listen to that inner voice, especially when it leads you into uncharted territory. My upbringing was not steeped in spirituality or holistic practices. We didn't meditate, light candles, or talk about energy. Everything I encountered in the world of personal development was new to me.

Yet, as I began to explore these concepts, doors opened. Opportunities appeared in unexpected ways. Each time I trusted my intuition, I was rewarded with growth, clarity, and connection.

One of the most impactful tools I discovered during this journey was intuitive journaling. This practice became a cornerstone of my personal and professional development, offering a way to connect deeply with my inner wisdom.

Intuitive journaling also became a space for reflection. I revisited entries and noticed patterns or recurring messages. This practice helped me identify areas of resistance or alignment in my life. For example, I once struggled with a decision to expand my business. My journal entries consistently pointed toward growth, even though it felt risky. Trusting that guidance led to one of the most significant milestones in my career—opening a second location.

In addition to journaling, I integrated other practices that enhanced my intuition. Meditation, spending time in nature, and mindfulness exercises became daily rituals. These activities helped me quiet the noise of the outside world and tune into my inner voice.

THE TOOL

Intuitive journaling is a simple yet transformative practice. It allows you to access the wisdom within and use it as a guide for your decisions, actions, and reflections. Here's how to begin:

Step 1: Create Your Sacred Space

- Choose a quiet place where you won't be interrupted.
- Set the mood with soft lighting, candles, or calming scents.
- Have your journal and a pen you love to write with.

Step 2: Connect With Your Intuition

- Begin with three deep breaths, inhaling through your nose and exhaling through your mouth.
- Set an intention: *Today, I am open to the messages my intuition has for me.*

Step 3: Write Without Censoring Yourself

- Start with the prompt: *What does my intuition want me to know today?*
- Let the words flow freely. Do not judge or edit yourself. Write until you feel complete.

The more you practice intuitive journaling, the stronger your connection to your inner wisdom will become. Over time, you'll find it easier to make decisions, overcome challenges, and align your life with your true purpose.

THE IMPACT OF INTUITION

Following my intuition has not only transformed my life but also inspired others to do the same. Over the years, I've had the privilege of coaching individuals who felt stuck, uncertain, or disconnected from their purpose. By encouraging them to trust their inner voice, I've witnessed incredible breakthroughs.

CLOSING THOUGHTS

Intuition is a powerful tool that resides within all of us. It's a source of guidance, clarity, and inspiration that can lead to profound success and fulfillment. By cultivating a practice of listening to your intuition, you open the door to endless possibilities.

Remember, the journey of intuitive success is not about perfection. It's about progress. Each step you take brings you closer to a life that feels authentic, meaningful, and aligned with your true self. So, take a moment today to pause, breathe, and listen. Your intuition is waiting to guide you toward your next extraordinary moment.

As you embrace this journey, know that every decision, no matter how small, holds the potential to transform your life. Trust in the process, and let intuition light the way to your greatest potential.

Deb Drummond, based in beautiful Vancouver, Canada, is a proud mother to her two favorite people, Chloae and Ocean, and a loving YaYa to Brynnlee and Kashton.

A trailblazer in entrepreneurship, Deb was among the first in Canada to establish health and wellness companies. She has built seven international businesses, inspired thousands worldwide, and has been featured in SUCCESS magazine 48 times. Her accolades include numerous nominations and awards for personal and professional achievements.

Deb is the visionary behind the Show Up Stand Up Speak Up, Yes You! movement, a televised project with a reach of over 350 million people, designed to inspire women and those that support women in celebrating International Women's Day. Her book, central to this movement, received acclaim at the 2024 Emmys Harvest Premiere Celebrity Gifting Suite and again at the Enchanted Gifting Suite for the 2025 Oscars.

With over 30 years of experience in high-performance training, Deb is a sought-after speaker, mastermind trainer, and personal coach. She has inspired audiences of over 20,000 to rise to their feet and personally coached more than 30,000 clients, helping them achieve optimal health and wealth.

Deb hosts the popular Mission Accepted podcast, featuring dynamic entrepreneurs, creatives, and media professionals sharing the real stories of entrepreneurship. She also created the Top Performance Day Planner and Tracker and founded Mission Accepted Media, producing anthologies and business-centric books.

Connect with Deb:

Website: https://www.debdrummond.com
LinkedIn: https://www.linkedin.com/in/DebDrummond/
Facebook: https://www.facebook.com/deborahldrummond/
Instagram: @deborahldrummond @debdrummond_official
@missionaccepted_media
YouTube: https://bit.ly/debs-channel

CHAPTER 16

HEALING HUMANITY

It's an Inside Job

By Jill Seabourne, CHt

MY STORY

Don't say anything else; you'll be exploited in the church.

And just like that, my eight-year-old self stopped talking about the things she knew.

Over the past two years, I learned how much of my true, authentic self I hid—not just from the world, but from myself. I began to notice it in small but meaningful ways: hesitating to speak up in conversations, avoiding sharing personal stories, and even downplaying my intuitive gifts when they naturally surfaced. These realizations came like puzzle pieces falling into place, showing me how fear had silently shaped my actions and interactions for years. That little girl inside me, afraid of what would happen if people knew who she was, silenced me all along.

Being intuitively gifted has been a part of my life for as long as I can remember. As a child, it meant having vivid dreams that later came true or sensing the emotions of people around me without them saying a word. I remember knowing when someone was upset, even if they wore a smile, or feeling compelled to offer comfort to a friend before they even voiced their troubles. As a young adult, I often knew things I couldn't explain, like when a friend would call or when a situation at work would take a sudden turn. These moments felt natural to me, but they often left others puzzled or amazed.

153

Frequently, I used my intuition without even realizing it. For me, it was just me being me. Occasionally, I said something to someone and saw the shocked look on their face—a look that told me I knew something I wasn't supposed to know. Sometimes, they came back days later, demanding to know who told me. I felt the fear rise within me, afraid to share my secret and tell them what my eight-year-old self confessed to my mom that day in the car: "Mom, I have ESP."

Deep inside, I've always known I'm here to help people heal. I remember a conversation with a mentor a few years back. I told her about this feeling I couldn't quite articulate, this deep knowing that I am, at my core, a healer. "Of course you're a healer. You're a medium," she said as if it were the most obvious thing in the world. But I explained it was more than that. "I know that as a medium and psychic, I help people heal through the messages I deliver from their loved ones. But this—this is something deeper, something I can't yet put into words."

Little did I know that the key to understanding this deeper part of myself would be healing my inner child wounds. The concept of the inner child refers to the part of us that retains the memories and feelings we experienced as children. This process began with acknowledging the pain I buried for so long—the fear, shame, and self-doubt instilled in me as a child. It wasn't easy to face those feelings, but I found solace and strength in journaling, meditation, and seeking guidance from trusted mentors. One significant moment was during a guided visualization exercise where I met my inner child, offering her the comfort and reassurance she always needed. These practices and the support of a sacred group of women helped me peel back the layers of protection I built and reconnect with my authentic self. That journey became my greatest testament to the healer I am.

I'm passionate about helping women like myself who are searching for something more in life—beyond the labels our families, religions, workplaces, and society assign to us. Girls are told who they're supposed to be from a young age. We're told to "be a good girl," "be polite," and "put others' needs before our own." These expectations can leave us feeling disconnected from our true selves.

Before I could help others on their journey to self-discovery, I had to walk that path myself. One pivotal moment came during a guided retreat when I was asked to reflect on a time I felt silenced or unseen. Memories of my eight-year-old self flooded back, and I realized how deeply that moment in the car with my mom shaped me. As I sat with those emotions, I felt a profound shift—a recognition that I had the power to rewrite my narrative. That experience became a catalyst for deeper exploration and healing. I remember asking myself, "How do I get there? How do I discover who I am at my core? Who is this healer inside of me?"

The answers began to unfold when I joined a sacred group of women in a yearlong program. This group, led by two knowledgeable and empathetic mentors, provided a safe space to share our experiences and support each other's healing journeys. At our first Zoom meeting, I saw the diversity among us. The women ranged in age from their 30s to their late 60s and came from various backgrounds across the United States. Some navigated broken marriages; others grieved the loss of a spouse. Each had her reasons for joining. For me, it was about reconnecting with that eight-year-old girl who had been silenced so long ago. I knew I had to tell her it was safe to share her truth.

The program was structured around monthly Zoom calls and quarterly in-person weekend gatherings. For our first weekend, our teacher suggested we bring a meaningful item to place on a co-created altar. I brought a photograph of myself when I was eight years old.

The living room had been transformed when we arrived at Michelle's home. In the center was a cloth representing the four directions, a bouquet of white roses, and a circle of white candles—one for each woman present. During the opening ceremony, we placed our chosen items on what Frances called a "living altar." Crystals, handwritten notes, and photographs filled the space, each representing something significant.

When I placed my photo on the altar, I began to weep. I cried for the little girl who had been eager to share her unique gift, only to be silenced. I cried for the parts of myself I kept hidden from family and friends. That weekend marked the beginning of deep inner child work for me—a journey of dissolving fears and reassuring that little girl, "It's safe now. No one will exploit you."

That was the turning point. I realized I had to start with myself to become the healer I felt called to be. For me, this meant establishing daily rituals of self-reflection and care. I began journaling to process my thoughts and emotions, making meditation a non-negotiable part of my daily life routine to connect with my inner self, and dedicating time to energy healing practices. As a hypnotherapist, working with a trusted colleague in hypnosis sessions also became a cornerstone, offering a safe space to confront and unravel deep-seated fears. Each step helped me rebuild my inner foundation, one small but meaningful action at a time. As the saying goes, "hurt people hurt people." We project our inner wounds onto the world. My eight-year-old self, afraid of being ostracized, turned me into someone who rarely shared her truth. If no one knew my secret, no one could judge me, take advantage of me, or impose their limiting beliefs on me.

But that weekend, I saw clearly that healing starts within. To truly be there for others and guide them on their journeys, I first had to go within and face the wounds I avoided. Only then could I fully step into the healer I was always meant to become.

THE TOOL

One of the most transformative tools I used along my journey was self-hypnosis. This powerful practice allows you to access your subconscious mind, the part of you that holds your deepest beliefs, emotions, and memories. Through self-hypnosis, you can gently uncover and address the blocks that may be holding you back, create new empowering beliefs, and cultivate a deeper connection with yourself.

The subconscious mind governs much of what we do on autopilot—from our habits and reactions to how we view ourselves and the world. Often, it's in the subconscious that limiting beliefs, old fears, and unresolved emotions reside. By entering a state of focused relaxation, self-hypnosis enables you to bypass the conscious mind's critical filter and communicate directly with the subconscious. This can lead to profound insights, healing, and transformation.

1.   Healing Inner Wounds: Self-hypnosis provides a safe space to revisit and heal past experiences, such as childhood memories or moments of emotional pain.

2.   Reducing Stress and Anxiety: By calming the mind and body, self-hypnosis can help you manage stress and bring a sense of peace.

3.   Enhancing Confidence and Self-Esteem: Self-hypnosis can reprogram limiting beliefs through positive affirmations and visualizations and help you reach your true potential.

4.   Improving Focus and Clarity: With regular practice, self-hypnosis sharpens your mental focus and helps you align with your goals and desires.

Here is a simple step-by-step guide to begin your self-hypnosis practice:

1.   Find a Quiet Space: Choose a place where you won't be disturbed. Sit or lie down in a comfortable position.

2.   Set an Intention: Decide what you'd like to focus on during your session. For example, you might want to release fear, boost self-confidence, or connect with your inner child.

3.   Relax Your Body: Close your eyes and take a few deep breaths. With each exhale, imagine releasing tension from your body. You can also do progressive relaxation, starting at your toes and moving upward, relaxing each part of your body.

4.   Enter a Hypnotic State: Visualize descending a staircase or counting down from ten, imagining yourself sinking deeper into relaxation with each step or number.

5.   Engage Your Subconscious: Once deeply relaxed, repeat affirmations or visualize your desired outcome. For instance, if your goal is to heal inner wounds, you might imagine a younger version of yourself surrounded by light and love.

6.   Stay in the Moment: Allow yourself to experience any emotions or insights that arise. Trust that your subconscious is guiding you toward healing and clarity.

7.   Return to Awareness: When ready, gently bring yourself back to the present moment. Count up from one to five; as you reach five, open your eyes, feeling refreshed and grounded.

8.   Reflect and Journal: Take a few moments to write down any thoughts, feelings, or insights from your session. This helps you integrate the experience and track your progress.

Tips for Success

•   Consistency is Key: Like any skill, self-hypnosis improves with practice. Aim to dedicate 10-15 minutes daily to your practice.

•   Be Patient: It's normal for your mind to wander at first. Gently guide your focus back to your intention.

•   Use Guided Scripts: If you're new to self-hypnosis, consider using pre-recorded meditations or creating your own tailored to your goals.

•   Combine with Other Practices: Pair self-hypnosis with journaling, meditation, or affirmations for even more profound results.

I remember one of my first experiences with self-hypnosis vividly. I struggled to confront a long-held fear of rejection. During a session, I visualized myself as a child, standing in front of a crowd, feeling afraid and exposed. As I guided myself deeper into the session, I imagined surrounding that child with a warm, protective light. I spoke to her compassionately, reassuring her that she was safe, loved, and free to express herself. I felt a profound sense of relief and empowerment when I emerged from the session. Over time, this practice helped me release the fear and thoroughly understand my truth.

Self-hypnosis is a gentle yet profound tool for personal growth and healing. It empowers you to take control of your inner narrative, heal past wounds, and align with your authentic self. Integrating this practice into your life can unlock new levels of self-awareness and transformation. Remember, the journey starts within, and self-hypnosis is a beautiful way to begin.

I still remember that afternoon in the car with my mom. We were stopped at the red light on the corner of Davis Highway and Brent Lane. As we sat there, my eyes caught a billboard sign across the street, towering between the dry cleaners and McDonald's: "Coming Soon ESP - Energy Services of Pensacola." Without hesitation, I turned to my mom and said, "Mom, I have ESP."

She glanced at me and then at the billboard and asked, "What do you mean you have ESP?"

At that moment, a voice in my mind cautioned: *Don't say anything else; you'll be exploited in the church.* It was as though the words were implanted directly into my consciousness. I paused and replied, "I just know stuff," before quickly changing the subject.

For years, I carried the weight of that moment, tangled with anger and fear. But now, looking back, I no longer feel those emotions. Instead, I see it as a defining memory, a point where my journey to understand myself began.

Jill Seabourne, CHt, is a certified transpersonal hypnotherapist, certified level 2 Quantum Healing Hypnosis Technique (QHHT) practitioner, certified cacao ceremony practitioner, and a trance medium healer and channel dedicated to helping individuals reconnect with their authentic selves. With a lifelong intuitive gift and a passion for empowering others, Jill specializes in guiding clients through transformative healing journeys that dissolve limiting beliefs and awaken inner potential.

Drawing on personal experiences of overcoming self-doubt and silencing, Jill combines modalities such as hypnosis, energy healing, and intuitive coaching to create personalized pathways for growth. She is passionate about helping women reclaim their truth and shed the societal labels that obscure their inner light.

Jill offers a safe and nurturing space for self-discovery through private hypnotherapy and trance medium healing sessions, group workshops, and her role as a teacher and mentor. Her work combines mystical insight, practical tools, and a heartfelt commitment to fostering meaningful transformation.

Connect with Jill:

Website: https://jillseabourne.com
Email: hello@jillseabourne.com
Facebook: https://www.facebook.com/people/Jill-Sebourne/61564744093812
Instagram: https://www.instagram.com/jillseabourne

CHAPTER 17

EMPOWERED SOUL ATTUNEMENT

Transformative Healing for Instant

Confidence and Clarity

By Nicole Pope, BSBA, Akashic and

Shamanic Evidential Medium

MY STORY

The night I found myself scrubbing vomit off my designer heels after escorting my inebriated boss home, I knew the universe was sending me a message: it was time to trade my spreadsheets for my soul's purpose.

But let me back up—because the path from metrics to mediumship wasn't exactly a straight line.

For two decades, I was the corporate world's golden child, armed with a Six Sigma Master Black Belt and a talent for turning chaos into order. Who knew being a professional problem-solver would become such a sought-after career path?

My reputation preceded me everywhere I went—financial services, healthcare, insurance, consulting, and private equity. I never needed to update my resume or suffer through awkward job interviews. Each new opportunity simply materialized through my growing network, like dominoes falling perfectly into place.

By any measuring stick, I crushed it. I worked shoulder-to-shoulder with C-suite executives, orchestrating multi-million-dollar transformations. Organizations thrived under my guidance—cutting costs, boosting growth, and hitting targets. Through data-driven process improvement, I healed these organizations from the inside.

While my resume painted a picture of success, my personal life crumbled beneath the demands of my career. On the surface, I had everything I was supposed to want—a loving husband, two incredible children, a beautiful house, and even the family dog. In reality, I became a neglectful spouse, an absent mother, and someone who lost sight of self-care, living on coffee and convenience food, canceling every gym session, and pushing my own health to the bottom of my endless to-do list. I was resentful, short-tempered, and restless. The fun, carefree person I once was vanished, replaced by someone I no longer recognized.

My mind screamed with desperation while my body sent undeniable signals—the constant knots in my stomach, the sleepless nights, the bone-deep exhaustion.

There has to be more to life than this.

The Universe answered my silent plea with a twist I never could've imagined.

The first whispers of change came through my eight-year-old son, who saw what the rest of us couldn't—shadow people moving through our home. They lived in our basement and lurked in the hallway outside our bedrooms. Though they never spoke, their presence made him so uncomfortable that he slept with his lights on, buried in his blankets. Chalking it up to an overactive imagination, I ignored his erratic behavior until he refused to be alone anywhere in our house. Knowing this was not normal and exhausting all other options, I sent an email to a local medium in November 2021, desperate for her advice.

"He's seeing spirits - actually seeing them with his eyes," she wrote back. "A child shouldn't have to deal with something like this. Just banish the spirits and turn off his power."

I stared at her email in disbelief. *The shadow people were real, and I had to banish them? What did she mean by turn off his power?*

I gave it my best shot. Unfortunately, my parenting books somehow missed the chapter on ghost-proofing. As one would expect from any amateur ghost-banishing, I failed miserably, and the shadow people continued to lurk. My son was more scared than ever, convinced they were demons out to steal his soul.

A few weeks later, I ran into the medium at an event. I explained her advice was not working and asked what else she could do to help us. She brushed me off in an annoyed tone, "You're a medium; why don't you deal with it yourself?"

Time froze.

Everything faded to black as I fixated on her.

What did she just say?

She responded to my dumbfounded expression, "What, you didn't know you were a medium?"

Eight words rewrote my entire reality.

It was as if a strike of lightning illuminated the dark shadows and desires of my soul. I'd always been drawn to mediumship, spending countless childhood hours glued to shows about connecting with spirit. But I'd only ever watched from afar until eight simple words invited this lifelong audience member to the stage.

The pull was magnetic. I found myself in her next beginner's mediumship class, my heart racing with possibility. And there, on that very first day, I connected to my first spirit.

In my mind's eye, a woman came into focus. "I see a woman dressed in red."

My teacher nodded.

As the spirit moved closer to me, I felt the urge to look down. As I gazed at my arms, my mind showed me a vision of them transforming into hers, with delicate yet wrinkled skin. I gasped and relayed, "I can see she is elderly and quite slender."

My teacher's eyes softened as she listened.

The elderly woman nudged me along, and my mind's eye suddenly flashed with a vision of her neighborhood. "I can see where she lived – it's a suburban street with sidewalks and green lawns. She is pointing to her flower garden… she seems really proud of it."

Slowly, the vision faded to black, and I could no longer see or feel her with me. I shrugged, certain I was imagining it all. "That's all I'm getting."

My teacher's smile grew warm as she spoke, "That is my departed neighbor. She loved the color red, and that garden was her pride and joy. You described her perfectly."

Tears rolled down my cheeks. *I really am a medium.* The flash of lightning ignited a roaring bonfire within my soul, awakening an insatiable hunger for spiritual knowledge.

And so began my spiritual binge era.

I became a metaphysical sponge, devouring books until my fingers were covered in paper cuts. Mediumship practice became a daily ritual, each session bringing through eerily specific details—the smell of a grandfather's cigar and a cherished memory of a winding drive through Hawaii in a red convertible. Tarot cards wore thin as they were consulted with every decision. My car became a rolling classroom, with spiritual podcasts playing endlessly on a loop. Weekends blurred together as I channeled universal energy, my hands tingling from newfound Reiki certifications. Even my dreams were filled with spirit guide whispers and symbols waiting to be decoded.

The more I worked with these metaphysical modalities, the more I noticed an innate knowing of what the answer was before it was revealed to me. I discerned the meaning of Tarot cards before I looked them up in the book, and I could detect someone's chakra imbalances before placing my hands on them. These moments of clarity felt unnerving with my data-driven background, where every decision required quantitative proof, presented in a flawless presentation reviewed by at least three levels of management.

But I noticed something crucial: unlike my emotional responses, which came tangled with fears and desires, my intuitive knowledge arrived void of emotion, logic, or expectations. Gradually, I learned how to differentiate my brain from my intuition. And when my brain was overbearing with anxious thoughts, I learned how to pause, tune in, and trust my intuition to illuminate the path forward.

The most startling discovery? When I tracked my intuitive hits against their outcomes, they were accurate. Every. Single. Time.

Less than a year after discovering spirit, my intuition told me it was time to open my spiritual business. Me, who still had a color-coded Excel to track my mediumship development progress. But that voice of inner knowing spoke louder than my fears. I was determined to follow where it led. With gritted teeth, I pushed through my nerves, launching a website, creating social media accounts, and trusting my intuition to set my prices. As always, my inner compass was right on course.

My business blossomed in ways I never imagined. When an invitation arrived to volunteer my services for a breast cancer fundraiser, my intuition shrieked yes. Standing before thirty eager faces, I discovered my passion for group readings. The perfect mentor arrived exactly when I needed her, first featuring me on her podcast and then inviting me to teach paid classes within her spiritual community.

Following my intuition's breadcrumbs, I hosted mediumship demonstrations at local venues, each event drawing more clients, students, and opportunities.

Every time I said yes to my inner voice, magic happened. My business's vibration drew in exactly what I needed next on my journey, expanding my impact while feeding the flames of my inner fire.

Let me take a moment to remind you—I orchestrated this spiritual awakening and entrepreneurial explosion while leading multi-million-dollar projects in my corporate job, regularly meeting with executives in my power suit and heels.

Though it was fun to live a double life, like the greats, eventually it caught up to me. My spiritual business flourished, demanding more time and energy, while my corporate workload remained extremely challenging.

You need to leave your job, my intuition whispered.

I can't walk away from everything I've fought so hard to build, my mind countered.

I repeatedly pushed these whispers aside, convinced the logic of my practical brain held more weight than my inner knowing.

But here's the thing about our intuition: the Universe has a way of turning whispers into thunderclaps when we refuse to listen.

In December of 2023, I attended my company's holiday party, drawn by the opportunity for face time with our executives. I slipped on my black sequined dress and stilettos, hopped in the car, and drove 90 minutes into the city. Upon arrival, I methodically worked the room, greeting executives, team members, and business partners. Despite the alluring martini bar with its elaborate concoctions, I stayed clear-headed and focused on making the right impression.

When my watch displayed ten o'clock, I remembered the old axiom: Nothing good happens after ten at company parties.

I feigned turning into a pumpkin, grabbed my coat, and headed toward the exit. In the lobby, I found an unlikely trio—my employee, my boss, and his boss (our senior executive). My employee's expression screamed HELP as he looked at me desperately.

My boss was sprawled in a lobby chair, five martinis past his limit, squinting at his phone as he failed to summon a ride home.

I inhaled deeply, knowing I was the only one who'd driven into the city. "It's fine," I heard myself say, "I'll drive him."

The senior executive met my gaze. "Are you sure?"

"Yes. He's on my way home. You two go back to the party. I'll bring my car around."

After hugs and thanks, I retrieved my car. I found him nearly unconscious on a bench outside the hotel. In stilettos on cobblestones, my 5'3" self somehow maneuvered my 6'5" boss into my car, then endured a twenty-minute drive punctuated by his retching at every stop. His ring camera undoubtedly captured the spectacle of me hauling him up the front steps, wrestling with his keys, and his platonic "I love you, Nicole!" before he stumbled inside.

Monday arrived, and with it, complete amnesia. My boss carried on as if nothing happened—no acknowledgment, no gratitude, no apology.

Fury simmered beneath my skin. *This man—who treated our holiday party like his 21st birthday—was my voice to senior leadership, wielding power over my bonuses, promotions, and future at the company.* At that moment, I saw the truth of the corporate clown car: beneath the pressed suits and polished presentations were people like him, who treated others as stepping stones, discarding lives while preaching company values. A system that rewarded those who could smile while stabbing backs, where empathy was weakness and ruthlessness was strength. I could never look at him, or corporate life, the same way again.

The universe's thunderclap was loud and clear. It broke through my clouds of self-doubt, and my intuition finally spoke louder than my excuses. I was done.

I crafted my escape plan. Six months gave me enough runway to build my business and savings, ensuring a secure transition. It also gave me time to protect my team—the good people caught in this corporate quagmire. I needed time to secure my employee's promotion before leaving. I also prepared my project co-lead, encouraging her to take center stage in our meetings so executives would see her as my successor. I refused to leave loose ends or abandoned allies behind.

Half a year vanished in a flash.

My intuition hummed with anticipation while one final item on my exit plan remained: giving my notice. I dreaded this conversation. I was their top talent, leading the company's most critical projects. They had no idea what was coming. Despite hours of meditation and rehearsed conversations, my nerves would not settle. I felt sick to my stomach.

The day I marked for my departure finally arrived. *It's now or never.* My heart pounded in my chest.

I anxiously knocked on the open door of the senior executive's office (you didn't think I'd give my notice to the martini king, did you?).

"Do you have a minute?"

He replied, "What's going on?"

I shut the door, held my breath, then exhaled. He looked concerned as I began, "I'm here to give you my notice." My eyes welled up.

His face transformed from worry to shock. "What do you mean?" he stammered, blindsided.

Tears burst forth like a broken dam; twenty years of emotions flooded out all at once. These weren't tears of sadness—they were washing away the hollow pursuit of promotions and prestige, the missed birthdays and family dinners, the exhausting game of corporate politics. They cleansed away all those years of sacrificing what truly mattered just to climb another rung on the ladder.

As I sobbed, the wave of tears baptized me into a new beginning—being reborn into a path that was unapologetically mine, full of joy, hope, and love.

He begged, bartered, and pleaded for me to stay but ultimately understood this was my decision to make. We agreed on a final date, and I slipped out of his office.

I donned my sunglasses, grabbed my badge and wallet, and descended twelve floors to the lobby. Through the city's morning rush, my tears dried into war paint as I walked. When I finally settled on a sunlit bench, I looked up. I sat directly in a sliver of sun that pierced through the canyon of dark skyscrapers. I closed my eyes, letting the warm sun reignite my soul's fire. I took a deep breath.

I'm free.

Six months after walking away from corporate life, the transformation is visible in every aspect of my world. Where tension and rushed goodbyes once filled our home, love and wonder flourish. My son, who once hid from the shadow people, confidently greets our spiritual visitors like the beloved family they are. Even my daughter's gifts emerged. She hears spirit whisper through her stuffed animals.

The change radiates through me as well—a light rekindled from within, visible to all who knew me before. That sliver of sunlight wasn't just illuminating my escape from corporate life; it was lighting the way to my true purpose. Now, as I guide others on their spiritual journeys, I measure success in moments of genuine connection, in awakened souls finding their path, and in the profound joy of living authentically. Looking back, I realize my son's gift didn't just transform his life; it transformed our entire family's destiny.

THE TOOL

When your inner compass feels clouded, and you're aching for clear direction and guidance, this attunement connects you with your highest self, helping you reclaim your divine wisdom and amplify your intuition.

Attunement Preparation

For this practice, you will need a journal, a pen, and a quiet place for deep connection.

Step 1: Creating a Sacred Space

Close your eyes, breathe deeply, and set your intentions. Below is how I open my sacred space, but trust your intuition to make it your own.

"Mother Earth, as I create this sacred space, I open to your ancient wisdom and ask that your energy flows through me.

Earth beneath me, wrap me in protection and anchor me in strength.
Water within me, unlock my intuition and wash away what no longer serves.
Fire before me, ignite my power and transform what's ready to shift.
Air above me, clear my mind and breathe in new understanding.

I invite my higher self into this sacred space to deliver messages with crystal clarity, illuminating my path. I trust in the wisdom that comes forward today, knowing it serves my divine purpose. I receive perfect information in perfect timing."

Step 2: Define Your Question

Take a moment to think about what you want clarity on right now. Feel into how this situation sits in your body and what beliefs you hold about it. When it feels right, write down your question in your journal. Be honest with yourself—simply express what you genuinely want to understand better.

Step 3: Receive Inner Wisdom

Breathe deeply and let your mind grow quiet. As your fingers trace these words, connect to their energy. Ask the questions below, or any other questions you feel called to explore. Pay attention to any feelings, thoughts, and emotions that bubble to the surface during this exercise.

Whatever comes through, whether it's a profound vision, a gentle whisper, a feeling in your body, or simply a moment of peace, is meant for you. Your experience is complete as it is. There's no need to question or judge what arrives; trust that it comes in precisely the right way, at precisely the right time.

Inner guidance to explore:

- What do I need to understand about this situation?
- What wisdom can I draw from past life experiences with similar challenges?
- What is my next aligned step?
- How will I recognize I'm on the right path?
- What will it feel or look like once I've overcome this?
- I ask you to attune me to the healing energies and past life integrations I need most right now.

Step 4: Reflect and Integrate

Pause to reflect on your experience. Write down any observations from the session and any inspired actions that resulted from connecting to your inner guidance.

Step 5: Close with Gratitude

Complete your sacred practice:

With deepest gratitude, this sacred circle is now closed.

Continue Your Soul Exploration

- Access the audio recording of this attunement and let my voice guide you through this sacred journey: https://mediumnicole.com/theintuitiveentrepreneur
- Rewrite your story and awaken your divine wisdom with a personalized session: https://mediumnicole.com/private-readings

Nicole Pope brings boardroom precision to spiritual transformation, helping others shatter the limitations of what they thought possible as an international Evidential Medium, Akashic Records reader, shamanic practitioner, spiritual mentor, energy healer, and host of the Empower Your Soul podcast.

With a grounded and discerning approach, Nicole artfully blends spiritual insight and practical wisdom to deliver profound results. Her signature method combines undeniable evidence from spirit with actionable guidance, empowering clients to achieve tangible breakthroughs in life, purpose, and potential.

Nicole's evidential mediumship readings provide healing and closure through powerful connections with loved ones. Her soul alignment sessions, which are a client favorite, are perfect for those seeking to shed self-limiting patterns and embody their authentic purpose. Through her business alignment sessions, entrepreneurs learn to leverage both spiritual wisdom and strategic insight to gain clarity and accelerate confidently on their path forward.

Known for cutting through complexity with refreshing directness, a dash of humor, and unapologetically fierce dedication to her client's growth, Nicole creates a space where the mystical becomes accessible and transformation becomes possible.

When she's not conducting sessions or mentoring others, she can be found enjoying chaotic moments with her family, chasing sunsets with her dog, or sharing spiritual insights (with plenty of expletives) on her podcast.

Connect with Nicole:

Website: https://MediumNicole.com
Empower Your Soul Podcast: https://mediumnicole.com/podcast
TikTok: https://www.tiktok.com/@mediumnicole
YouTube: https://www.youtube.com/@MediumNicole

Instagram: https://www.instagram.com/MediumNicoleA/
Facebook: https://www.facebook.com/106085625853564
Free Gift: 5 Signs Your Business is Out of Alignment:
https://mediumnicole.com/free-businessalignment

CHAPTER 18

CONVERSATIONS WITH NATURE

Heal Burnout and Cultivate Slow Living

By Shannon Mitchell, Herbalist

MY STORY

The plants spoke to me long before I became an herbalist.

It took me a long time to admit I heard their messages. It took me longer still to announce, in perfect seriousness, to a room of herbalism students that I talk to plants, and they talk back.

Yet, I know to the core of my being, in the deepest marrow of my bones, that the natural world is profoundly connected to us. It's silently waiting, longing for us to rebuild the relationship we've lost in our fast-paced modern world.

While I began my formal study of plant medicine over four years ago, I first heard their songs as a child.

I was six the first time I felt them.

It was in our backyard garden alongside my mom, hands deep in the loamy soil, knees sinking into the cool, malleable earth, that I understood nature had sentience.

While I didn't have the words for it, a steady certainty spread through my chest as I peered at the proud, beaming sunflowers lining our fading, gray fence. They seemed to beckon to me. I heard their collective voice in my mind.

Come closer, tender heart. Let us get a better look.

Their radiant energy floated down to dance along my skin and filled me with warm delight as I studied them carefully.

We see your sorrows. We are here, always watching, always with you. Come to us whenever you feel lost or alone.

My heart ached at the gift they offered, a soft breeze stroking my cheek, as if in confirmation.

The plants were my friends and allies, each with a personality that called me. They were all unique and had their own distinct gifts and mysterious wisdom.

The bewitching, sharp-eyed seriousness of the roses underneath our bay window made me curious yet wary, their medicine more biting.

You may admire our beauty but respect our thorns. See our protection and approach us slowly. We love deeply yet require space when sharing breath.

I often kept my distance, something that followed me into adulthood. I avoided working with rose for many years, unable to pinpoint why.

When I finally did, her heart and sacral medicine helped me heal the shame around my sexuality, something I had not been previously ready to face. She knew I would need her someday, so she waited.

That is the divinity of the plants.

They know us more intimately than we could ever imagine. They understand how to heal us. The right medicine for the right person at exactly the right time. When you're a child, before you're taught to feel shame about being different, or Western culture encourages you to scrutinize things like intuition, you know this in your heart.

There's a special kind of magic to wild things and places.

The mischief, mystery, and magnificence of nature are a mirror to us.
They're a part of us.
They are us.

Until we're told we're separate, superior, or too civilized to believe in such things and we forget where we came from.

As I got older, I lost touch with my intuition entirely. I abandoned that deep knowing to feel safe in a chaotic household and fit into the fray of uncertainty and self-consciousness that epitomizes teenage friend groups. Self-trust dissolved as my desperate need to be liked eclipsed the voice of my soul.

Culture told me who I was supposed to be and what I was supposed to want, what would make me lovable, acceptable, and worthy.

I was twelve when I started watching MTV music videos before catching the bus. I was mesmerized by the women moving across the screen.

I wish I looked like that. God, why am I so ugly? Why did you make me look like this?

I thought about my auburn hair, the gleaming braces, unflattering glasses, and oversized nose I hadn't yet grown into.

I am hideous. I will never be beautiful. I will never be as good as they are.

I rejected my true self and suffocated my inner flame, that kernel of power and connection to truth, in exchange for external validation.

I felt worthless and misunderstood, a yawning chasm of emptiness I tried to fill with anything I could. I became obsessed with proving my worth, especially to men, traveling, and achieving to feel like I mattered. It kept me in a pattern of toxic relationships and self-destructive behaviors for almost a decade.

Eventually, though a conventional life never interested me, the exhaustion of making little money waitressing led me to seek a more stable paycheck.

I unknowingly chose something familiar to the chaos I'd become accustomed to, going into youth mental health. I was constantly activated and plagued by compassion fatigue.

I oscillated between constant anxiety and numbing dissociation, falling into spirals of self-criticism and rejection, berating myself internally.

What have you accomplished? Look at these successful people. Gabby Bernstein had an empire by the time she was 30. You'll never be like her. You will never be good enough.

I never sat still, always moving or trying to achieve something, until one day, that small whisper of knowing, the thread that once connected me to the plants, and by extension to myself, awoke.

A Turning Point

"Your blood tests came back completely normal."

I readjusted the phone between my ear and shoulder, staring at the double monitors on my overcrowded desk, not absorbing what was on the screens.

"You tested negative for Lyme and immunodeficiencies. Nothing came back abnormal, so we can rule those out." She paused, awaiting my response.

I felt a small tug in the back of my mind as I chewed over what she'd said. A gentle voice spoke to me.

You already knew that, though, didn't you?

"Is there anything else that could be causing it?" I pressed.

Silence fell as she considered. "It may be lifestyle-related and worth exploring. You mentioned you're working a lot of hours; it could result from exhaustion. Stress could be another contributor. Are you resting enough?"

A small, knowing smile tugged at the corner of my mouth.

"Maybe not," I said sheepishly, conceding it could be a factor.

"Well, you might want to start there. Overexertion can impact your immune system and make you more susceptible to illness. In the meantime, you can take Ibuprofen as needed and call me if anything changes."

The exasperated thoughts flooded my mind as I thanked her for the information and tossed my phone into the mess of paperwork before me.

Shocking. Once again, Western medicine suggests pain meds. Why is that always the answer?

The call left me feeling a mixture of deflation and shame. Deflation because I didn't feel relieved with the results and shame because I thought the joint pain and fatigue I'd been suffering would've been easier to deal with if they were explained by a diagnosis.

Then there would at least be a tangible, namable reason I felt so numb, stretched so thin, and completely exhausted, too tired to do anything I enjoyed.

I leaned back in my chair, studying the far corner of my office. A few shimmering cobwebs glimmered there, catching the last rays of afternoon sunlight cascading across the walls.

It wasn't her fault, but her words echoed in my head anyway.

Your results came back normal.

Something else, then. Something deeper.

But I knew.

I knew before I hung up the phone it was burnout. Knew before she asked me if I was resting enough, knew deep down before she even told me the test results.

It was something I avoided because I didn't want to face everything underneath it, despite knowing emotional pain would eventually manifest sickness in the body.

I thought about how tired I felt. How I always thought my happiness would be found in the "next thing."

At the time, I worked for an abusive, unprofessional boss I didn't like or respect, managing a high-conflict team, and completely enmeshed in a dysfunctional, co-dependent relationship.

I didn't want to admit I was overextended and not setting any real boundaries because otherwise, I would have to do the painful work of changing. It was easier to think I was a victim of life rather than develop enough self-love, accountability, and courage to disappoint others by prioritizing myself.

Yet, I knew if I continued to ignore my body, I'd eventually develop an actual disease, so I decided to set up an intuitive session with my dear friend and psychic medium, Deb.

"Are you studying herbalism?"

It was one of the first things she asked after closing her eyes. Her hand was on her heart, and her head tilted slightly to the side, a small furrow appearing on her brow.

I leaned forward in my chair, studying her still-closed eyes, and considered. I wasn't, but in her words, the second session in three years she'd said them, that small part of me, the wild, forgotten essence of knowing, began to stir, perking its eager ears.

"Currently, I'm not, but I've been wanting to for years. The last time I saw you, you told me my guides said it was something I should pursue," I answered.

She nodded her head knowingly. "Okay, yes, they really want you to find a teacher. They are saying you would find a lot of value and healing in that."
It was confirmation enough.

Even underneath the layers of self-denial and numbness, I still believed in the universe, signs, and the spirit world.

I knew it was time.

Healing Through Nature and Returning to Earth Pace

I sought an herbalism teacher for a year when I finally found her, the director of the School of the Sacred Wild. Along with practical applications of Western herbalism, my apprenticeship introduced me to plant spirit medicine and how to communicate with plants to support my own and others' healing.

Excited and feeling a "yes" I hadn't in years, I watched the first three-hour opening ceremony on my living room floor. Propped between a chair and my hand-me-down coffee table, I sat cross-legged, leaning into the screen expectantly, hands clasped around a steaming mug of burdock tea, listening carefully to each word.

One of the initial lessons Marysia taught, along with the plant meditation, was regarding the dismemberment or disembodiment that tends to permeate tech-dominated, nature-disconnected cultures.

"In the West, we move into our heads, essentially living from the head instead of the heart, cutting ourselves off from our intuition and ability to discern from our hearts."

She continued.

"We rarely slow down enough to know what's happening in the body, let alone access deeper healing. It's very difficult for us to find 'Earth pace' when we're stuck in fight or flight or the constant productivity capitalism encourages."

I didn't realize how true that was for me until my physical symptoms became impossible to ignore.

After her lecture, she asked us to drop into several guided meditations with different herbs. We began with sweet, grounding burdock, sipping the tea slowly and bringing bodily awareness to its medicine.

Marysia provided brief prompts throughout.

"Notice where this beautiful plant ally wants to be in your body, how it feels to ingest her."

I swallowed and waited.

Slowly, I felt a cooling, descending energy move through my body as mental pictures of thick taproots formed in my mind. I was pulled downward, lovingly anchored to the Earth, feeling safe and present. I remained there, solely focused on the feeling of safety, as if in a trance.

Eventually, Marysia's voice cut back in.

"Bring your awareness to your heart, asking this ally if she has any other messages for you. Expressing deep gratitude for all her beautiful medicine."
I opened my eyes, bringing myself back to my body.

That first plant meditation was a homecoming for me. It was like clearing thick layers of fog, remembering something I'd long forgotten yet could not name. Through the plants, I rebuilt the lost connection with my intuition, the original chord to nature in the first place.

I began hearing her again, listening to her messages, and self-healing with her wisdom and guidance. I learned how to recognize my needs and make decisions from a place of safety and true discernment, which is one of the biggest components of self-healing and slow living—feeling safe enough to do so.

I worked on my self-abandonment wounds and started coupling herbs with seasonal shifts and energies. I introduced rituals, practices, and recipes that supported my cycles, prioritizing three things throughout: rest, connection, and time spent in nature.

I started saying "no," strengthening my boundaries, learning to sit with silence and difficult emotions.

Although to me it felt ground-breaking to rediscover the language of nature, for Indigenous peoples, plant spirit communication has long been integrated into their cultural practices, spiritual beliefs, and ethical ethos. While this is a healing modality and lifestyle many in the Western herbalism community are beginning to discover, for most of human history, life revolved around the land and the cyclical seasons of nature.

It's only in the last few thousand years that we've become this disconnected from the Earth, less self-sufficient, and ever reliant on the conveniences of technology, not understanding the true impact of overconsumption.

Working with the plants transforms us wholly. It helps us cultivate slower living, deeper empathy and reverence for life, sourcing, and how we treat the natural environment, acknowledging the lineages these practices come from and reducing harm through regenerative products, practices, and sustainable solutions for future generations.

And since in the West, we've forgotten a lot of these core assumptions, I've designed a tool to help you connect with nature and start to remember.

THE TOOL

I would like to share a simple yet powerful practice with you to begin connecting with nature on a deeper level.

In this short plant meditation, I walk you through how to meet them through quiet observation. This can be done with any living plant (including house plants!) and does not require any additional materials, although you can grab a journal and pen if you'd like to record what you receive.

Begin by choosing the plant you'd like to connect with. It can be one you're already familiar with or a plant you're feeling called to. Find a comfortable position, sitting next to the plant of your choosing.

Take five slow, deep belly breaths to ground yourself into the moment and space, moving yourself into a receptive state. This will help you receive any messages they may have for you.

Introduce yourself to the plant, speaking your name out loud and sharing your desire to learn from the spirit of this ally. Thank this plant for summoning you to connect.

It may feel a little silly at first—that's okay! It takes time to move from the thinking, logical brain to the intuitive senses. Nature is patient and will not judge or laugh at you.

Study the way this plant looks before closing your eyes and imagining you are standing in a special place in nature. This can be any landscape that resonates with you, noticing the details of your surroundings and how it feels to be there. If your mind begins to wander, gently bring yourself back to your intention.

Bring the picture of your plant back to your mind, envisioning it floating before you. Notice how it wants to appear and share your desire to learn from its wisdom, asking it to share its gifts.

Allow yourself to remain here in stillness, waiting and listening to its voice. You may experience subtle sensations in different areas of the body or receive messages in the form of pictures, words, or beings in your mind. You could also experience profound emotions you did not know existed or where they stem from.

Or you may experience nothing at all.

All of this is okay.

Nature teaches in many ways, including through curiosity or a draw to certain plants, feeling a preference for a particular herb, or attaching sentimental memories to parts of nature.

Try to remain neutral and open without letting the logical side of your brain take over and make judgments like "It's not working" or "I'm doing it wrong." Not all plants will resonate with you and that's okay, it just means it isn't the medicine you currently need, and there will be different plants you connect with more.

Ask this plant if there are any other messages it would like to share before slowly coming back into your body. Bring your awareness to the heart, thanking this plant for connecting with you.

When you return, feel free to write about your experience or simply sit in silence, soaking in the magic.

This practice can be repeated infinitely with any plant or as a tea ceremony. You can ingest your (non-toxic) herbs in water as I did in my apprenticeship, following their movement through the body, as another wonderful way to connect.

Shannon Mitchell is a folk herbalist, facilitator, and writer. Her business, Shannon Mitchell Wellness, uses the transformative power of nature to support clients in developing practical, self-guided approaches to healing. Through her work, she teaches others how to rebuild their relationship with plant medicine, reconnect with the earth, and slow down enough to integrate herbalism and self-healing into daily, seasonal living.

When she's not talking to plants, Shannon is feverishly working on projects or collecting hobbies. You might find her cloistered in her garden, hosting lively dinner parties, cursing renovations on her 1800s farmhouse, or catching early morning flights to new places with her partner, always ready for the next adventure.

Her other love, writing, can be found on her Substack, Unraveling with Shannon and Medium, Shannon Mitchell Writes, where she explores the intersection of healing, relationships, culture, and existential dread with humor and vulnerability.

Connect with Shannon:

Substack Newsletter: https://shannmitch.substack.com
Writing on Medium: https://medium.com/@ShannonMitchellWrites
Website: https://www.shannonmitchellwellness.com
Instagram: https://www.instagram.com/shangrowsplants

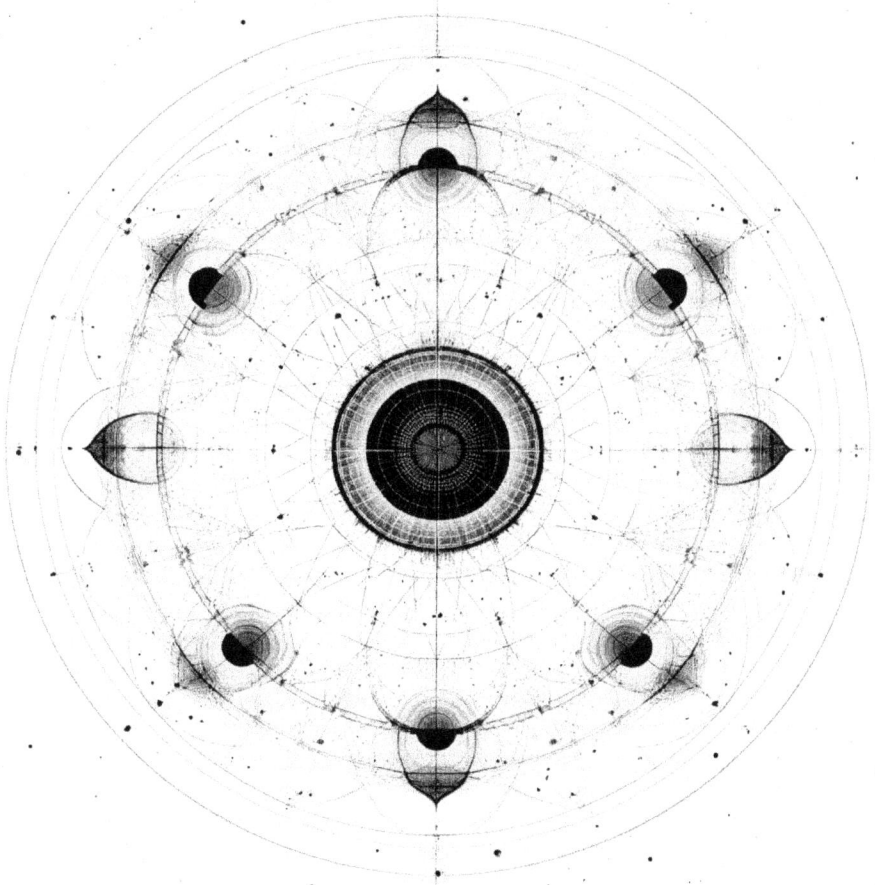

CHAPTER 19

In Service of the Divine

Breaking Out of the Small Business Paradigm

By Bradford W. Tilden, MM, CMT, UWT

For me, being an intuitive entrepreneur is not a career. It's a way of life. All I've ever done is listen, follow my heart, trust, and take action, following the divine plan as it unfolds before me.

I've highlighted some of the key turning points in my life that got me to where I am today. All of which were based completely on following my intuition.

This is my fifth book with Brave Healers. This is what I get for following my intuition! For a better understanding of the breadth of my intuitive entrepreneurial reality, I encourage you to read my other chapters as well.

In "Universal White Time: Leveraging the Power of Divine Light and Love for Authentic Healing and Awakening" from *The Energy Medicine Solution: Mind Blowing Results For Living An Extraordinary Life* I share my journey of connecting with the extraterrestrial healing modality, Universal White Time Gemstone Healing of which I'm now a leading teacher in North America.

In "The Secret of Humming: Harnessing the Power of Your Voice for Personal Transformation" from *Bytes of Light: Evolving Leadership for the Spiritual Entrepreneur,* I share my emergence as a master vocal sound healer with quartz crystal singing bowls.

In "Your Brave Spiritual Upgrade, Manifesting Magic During Any Challenging Conversation" from *How To Be Brave: Self-Healing Tools for Love Warriors*, I share my struggles and triumphs using Universal White Time Energy Healing to elevate my energy and spiritual presence.

And in "Mastery of Past Lives, How to Accelerate Your Conscious Awakening" from Shaman Heart Volume 3: *We Are The Ones We've Been Waiting For*, I share my experience on an author's journey to Peru and the intersection with integrating my past lives as a Lemurian Priest-Healer.

MY STORY

"Bradford, what do you think you're doing?" The question was delivered more like a loving judgment.

"What am I looking at here? Two study periods, pottery class (!), and only one advanced placement course?"

I grinned and shrugged as she reflected my second-semester junior year class schedule back to me.

"With your grades and extracurricular activities, you can get into any college you choose."

The extra-long red acrylic nails clicked avidly about her computer keyboard. Her matching gaudy bobble earrings that screamed of the fashion whims of the late 90s wiggled with excitement. Her postmodern spin on the classic beehive hairdo nodded in agreement.

My guidance counselor was a force to be reckoned with.

I assumed I'd go to college but hadn't given it much thought. I had no idea what I wanted to be or what I wanted to do. I just knew I loved playing the piano, writing music, and that I was very smart.

"Let's see. Harvard, Yale, Brown. You should definitely have these on your list."

I covered a yawn with my hand as she rattled off the names of the Ivy Leagues.

"Oh, what about Amherst College?"

My ears perked up. I leaned forward. I hadn't heard of Amherst College before.

"Amherst College is ranked as one of the top liberal arts colleges in the country. Oh, and it says here they have no core curriculum."

No core curriculum? I can take any classes I want? I have to check this place out.

That summer I did what every aspiring incoming high school senior did and visited my top choices. Harvard? I found the energy too pretentious. Brown? I felt lost in the vastness. Yale? Eh, Maybe, but it felt congested.

As soon as I set foot on the Amherst College campus, my entire head tingled.

This is the one.

I applied early decision to Amherst College. When I received my acceptance letter the following January, I tossed the other partially-completed college applications in the trash with a smirk. Amherst was the only school I applied to. I intuitively knew I was meant to go there.

This was the first domino.

I made two significant connections at Amherst College. The first happened on the first day of orientation. Freshly pumped with adrenaline from watching my parents drive away, I practically floated toward my assigned meeting point, filled with the possibilities within this newfound freedom.

It was only the awkwardness of meeting 20 equally emancipated strangers, my "orientation pod," that kept me tethered to my body. Sitting cross-legged in a circle on the manicured lawn, I observed varying degrees of emotion ranging from anxiety to hopeful expectation, haughtiness to meekness on the fresh faces of my fateful freshman peers.

My eyes locked on another's. Her expression was as intense and inquisitive as mine. I looked down and noticed a pride ring necklace hanging around her neck. Instinctively, I knew she saw my matching pride ring necklace. At that instant, we both smiled. Our eyes communicated knowingness. Our smiles became stretched grins.

When the pod dispersed, we walked away, instant friends. Out and proud.

The second connection was made during the second semester of my senior year.

"Could you pick up the visiting pianist from the train station?" the music professor asked me. "I think you and he will really get along."

Oh, so he's a fag like me.

"Sure thing!" I dutifully complied as the stage manager for a postmodern interpretation of Schubert's Winterreise song cycle.

Wow, I'm getting a personal introduction to a professional pianist from New York!

My professor was right. We hit it off.

He insisted on taking me to an expensive Italian restaurant before returning to campus. We chatted about music and men over dinner. When we arrived at the guest faculty housing, he invited me inside.

"I'm really sore and stiff from the train. Will you give me a massage?" he asked.

I don't think this is part of my stage manager duties, but sure, why not?

"Okay, but I've never given a massage before," I qualified.

"That's fine," he assured me as he plopped a bottle of lotion from his bag in my hand and proceeded to undress.

What followed was a completely intuitive full-body massage. I let my highly developed classical piano-trained fingers dictate where to go, how much pressure to use, how long to apply the pressure, and how to release the pressure. I was balanced, centered and relaxed when I finished. It was a wonderful feeling of satisfaction.

"You're telling me you've never given a massage before?" he asked incredulously.

"No. I haven't."

"Bradford, that was the best massage I have ever received, and I've gotten massages from people all over the world." His sincerity was palpable.

"I guess I have a knack."

He and I are still close friends today. He's the reason I went to massage school after my one-year fellowship as the assistant choral director at Amherst College.

When almost every other person in my graduating class scampered off to pre-med, pre-law, or was recruited by one of the many investment banking firms whose scouts pecked about our campus like greedy vultures, I went to a local community college to obtain a massage therapy certification.

Irrational? You bet.

Intuitive? 100%

One more domino falls.

A few months after graduating from massage school, I received a call from my out and proud friend I met at orientation.

"Hey Brad, my father bought me a two-unit house in the Castro as a graduation present. How would you like to move out to San Francisco and live with me?"

The perks of going to Amherst College.

Without any savings, without a job lined up, with only a promised place to stay, I arrived in San Francisco in January 2005.

Irrational? You bet.

Intuitive? You get the idea.

Another big domino came tumbling down.

My housing situation turned out to be temporary. My friend populated her second unit with a harem of lesbians who knew how to party. She gave me a generous three weeks to find another place to live.

Having originated in San Francisco, Craig's List was a viable and respectable source of housing resources at the time. I responded to an ad for a gay-friendly roommate that led me on an adventure up the steep hill of Upper Market Street above the Castro.

The interview didn't go so well. If there was anything like too gay, I found it in that apartment.

On the way back, however, I noticed a fork in the road. I paused and felt the energy of each option. Even though it looked uninviting, my intuition pulled me down this path less traveled.

After a few blocks, I spotted a little black rectangular sign swaying gently above the entrance to a small business.

The sign read, "Shift Happens."

You're telling me!

I knocked, knocking over another domino in the process.

"Come in!"

This was the day I met Terry Yoder, a psychic medium.

In many ways, Terry was a gatekeeper. He offered his space for me to rent for massage clients. He encouraged me to facilitate a weekly healing circle after I became Reiki and White Time attuned where I discovered I'm a natural at facilitating guided meditations. He introduced me to the person who opened my life to sound healing.

Because of Terry, I bought my first crystal bowl. My intuition said "yes" when Terry invited me to accompany him to San Luis Obispo, where he was doing readings at a psychic fair.

As soon as I arrived at the fair, my eyes shot right to the only crystal bowl in the space of 40 vendors. I had been hunting for a crystal bowl since I discovered their existence at the sound healing school.

I zipped up to the booth.

"Why is this bowl so cheap?" I asked, pointing to the $111 price sticker on the 14" classic frosted bowl.

"This bowl is a primordial diamond. It was created when they were still perfecting the casting process. See that nipple on its side? That defect causes the bowl to fluctuate in both pitch and volume. Many people find that undesirable."

"I'll take it."

This bowl became my teacher. Its "defect" disciplined me to master microtonal vocal frequency adjustments when toning with it. Interestingly, I've never encountered another "primordial diamond."

More dominos fall, leading me along an elegant interconnected path the complexities of which are only known to the divine architect of my soul's design. The more I surrender to my intuition, the more doors open, opportunities present themselves, and the structure of my true work begins to crystallize.

My intuitive entrepreneurial spirit leaped right into every new opportunity. I began offering innovative combinations of music, massage, sound, and UWT gemstone healing as professional healing experiences. My life was in the "start-up" phase. Not caring about the risks and not knowing the rewards, I quit my day job and became an instrument of the divine.

One day, my partner at the time (who was also my self-proclaimed manager) brought me an opportunity to perform my piano music at a conference in Santa Cruz without pay.

"You really ought to take this gig," he said.

"Why? What's the conference about?"

"I'm not sure, but I have a feeling."

We were at an impasse.

"Let's let the pendulum decide," I suggested.

I rarely consult a pendulum, but something told me to pick it up.

With the pendulum dangling motionless from my outstretched hand, I said, "Show me the energy surrounding this event for me."

Wide-eyed, we both gasped as the pendulum whipped wildly around the little ball fulcrum pinched between my thumb and index fingers. The pendulum spun clockwise like a propeller parallel to the floor.

Still muttering under my breath, I nearly toppled over the big floor display sign reading "Dr. Laurie Moore, Animal Communicator" outside the double doors to the partitioned conference room with my cumbersome electric keyboard case. I huffed as I dragged it up to the stage past several rows of random people cutting through the cloud of idle mumbling and expectant chatter.

A skinny middle-aged woman with endearingly unkempt, long, dark, wavy hair bounced toward me with the energy of an eager child.

"You must be Bradford. Nice to meet you! I'm Dr. Laurie Moore. Thank you for coming. I'm excited to hear you play." Laurie's smile beamed. Her sky-blue eyes glowed as if the sun itself was behind them.

"I'm going to open with a meditation and then some interpretive dance."

What have I gotten myself into?

From the stage, I watched in awe as this woman bore her authentic soul through movement in front of a crowd of complete strangers.

Then it was my turn.

I played a set of original classical piano music from my album Behind the Surface. To say the audience was receptive is an understatement. A visible transformation took place in the room. Joe Shmo from Idaho now appeared to be an Arcturian. To his left was an Earth Angel. Behind her was an elf. Two rows back, I swear, was an ET sitting next to a leprechaun, and so on. I saw the higher selves superimposed over every human.

Then they started sharing their experiences my music engendered. That moment, I learned unequivocally my music heals.

This is the type of high-vibrational audience Dr. Laurie attracts. She and I became lifelong friends.

The many dominos from attending that event included my becoming her resident healer/musician at several spiritual retreats in Hawai'i.

One of my favorite memories is giving her an intuitive gemstone layout as a thank-you.

We'd just finished a round of capture the flag. The other participants headed to the cabin for personal reflection time, enjoying the private beach along the tranquil Lanai coastline.

Laurie lay on a patch of lush grass under a large plumeria tree. The many flowers along the low-hanging branches blessed our sacred space with their enchanting fragrance.

I intentionally selected and ritualistically placed gemstones from my master kit over the major energy points along the central axis of her body. When I reached the solar plexus none of the stones on hand felt correct.

What to do?

There at her side was a single fallen plumeria flower in perfect condition.

Yes. Of course.

I plucked it from the grass and placed it delicately on the center of her willpower. After 20 minutes of angelic toning with an 8" bowl, I removed the stones and flower.

She sat up with a look of wonder spread across her face.

"I've been disconnected from my solar plexus for years," she emphasized.

"As soon as you placed the flower there, I felt energy surging there. It feels completely whole and integrated!"

"Intuition is the language of vibration. Anything can be used to heal as long as it has the right frequency," I told her.

Months later, she confided in me that she picked up her guitar again after a long period of neglect and got back into singer/songwriting thanks to that one healing session in Lanai.

This is but one of the many living testaments to the power of my intuitive healing abilities.

Dominos continue to fall to this day.

THE TOOL

It's never too late to start making intuitive decisions to build the life of your dreams, your life of joy. If you say you're an artist but haven't picked up a paintbrush in months or years, if you say you're a writer and you haven't put pen to paper for a while, if you want to work for yourself, but you haven't taken any action towards making that a reality, now is the time.

At this time of ascension, all people, beings, and energies in the known universe support your mission. We want you to succeed. Joy is the highest expression of the love vibration. If ever there was an obligation to yourself, it's to manifest your joy in this lifetime. Doing so fulfills your soul's purpose and catapults you into a higher frequency.

You don't need to quit your job. You don't need to do anything extreme.

If you can't find time, make time. Create a time-container to pursue your passion.

All you need to do is set a timer for 30 minutes and work towards your goal once a day for a minimum of 30 minutes. Start small because a little becomes more and more is what you manifest to support your intuitive entrepreneurial lifestyle.

If you're unsure which direction to go in, shift your mindset to focus not so much on what you do but on who you are in your authentic soul expression. Don't consider yourself a small business owner. Don't go into business for yourself. Instead, work for the Universe.

Make the divine plan your business plan.

You've built up divine credit from your past lives, mastering the gifts you brought to this lifetime.

These gifts are easily identifiable.

What are you most passionate about?

What brings you the most joy and fulfillment?

If you're hesitant to live your joy, here are a few effective core belief affirmations to build confidence:

- I believe in myself, have faith in the universe, and trust I will always be provided for.
- I always have more than enough money than I need.

- I lead a prosperous life doing what brings me the greatest joy for a living.
- I am an instrument of the divine.
- I align my will with the divine will of my higher self to give and receive love, healing, and abundance on this sacred day.

Stay in the present. The ever-evolving future is unfathomable to our limited human consciousness. Trust in the moment and allow the unfolding to occur. Don't limit yourself with what you think you need/want/should do. The Universe has great plans for you when you align with your divine joy.

Good luck to you. I am here for you. I believe in you.

Use this link https://calendly.com/crystalmusichealing/20min to schedule a free 20-minute consultation, but only if you are intuitively guided to. I would love to hear what brings you joy and discover what dominos we can knock over together.

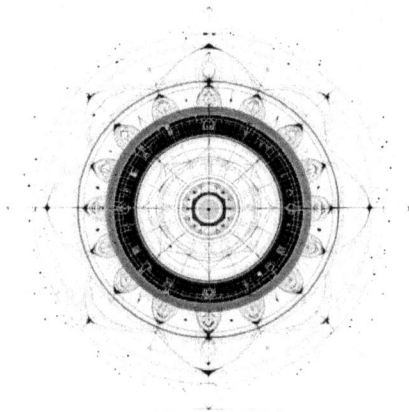

Bradford W. Tilden MM, CMT, UWT is an international best-selling author, composer, pianist, angelic shaman, and master intuitive vibrational healer who specializes in sound, crystal, gemstone, and Universal White Time healing. He's one of North America's pioneering UWT gemstone and energy healing teachers. He graduated magna cum laude from Amherst College in 2002, attended the Globe Institute of Sound and Consciousness in San Francisco in 2006, and received a master's degree in music composition from UMASS, Amherst in 2014.

Bradford founded the Lemurian School of Intuitive Natural Healing in 2008. LSINH's (pronounced "listen") mission is to develop one's intuition while utilizing the power of sound and crystals to become an effective healer for oneself and the world. It's derived from the knowledge of the ancient Lemurian civilization, as revealed to him by his UWT crystal master guides, past life remembrance as a Lemurian priest-healer, and through his work with Lemurian seed crystals.

As a sacred sound ceremonialist, his music and live sound journeys are divinely orchestrated collaborations. Bradford vocally channels authentic angelic, galactic, and indigenous shamanic healing frequencies. Find his music on all the major streaming platforms. Support his musical artistry at https://bradfordwtilden.bandcamp.com

Bradford awakens the greatness in people through inspiration, education, and the activation of mastery within. Visit https://www.CrystalMusicHealing.com to learn more about UWT, LSINH, and all the remote healing services and products he offers, including spiritual upgrades. Contact him for music/sound healing commissions or to host a class. He'll travel anywhere in the world to teach. Book a free 20-minute consultation here: https://calendly.com/crystalmusichealing/20min. He'd love to hear from you.

When he's not hiking or visiting family on Cape Cod, you can find him playing the piano or talking to his crystals at home with his husband in Cheshire, Connecticut.

Connect with Bradford:

Linktree: https://linktr.ee/bradfordtilden
Facebook: https://Facebook.com/CrystalMusicHealing
Instagram: https://instagram.com/BradfordTilden
YouTube: https://youtube.com/MuseOfAquarius
LinkedIn: https://www.linkedin.com/in/bradfordtilden
TikTok: https://www.tiktok.com/@theshirtlessshaman
Patreon: https://patreon.com/bradfordtilden

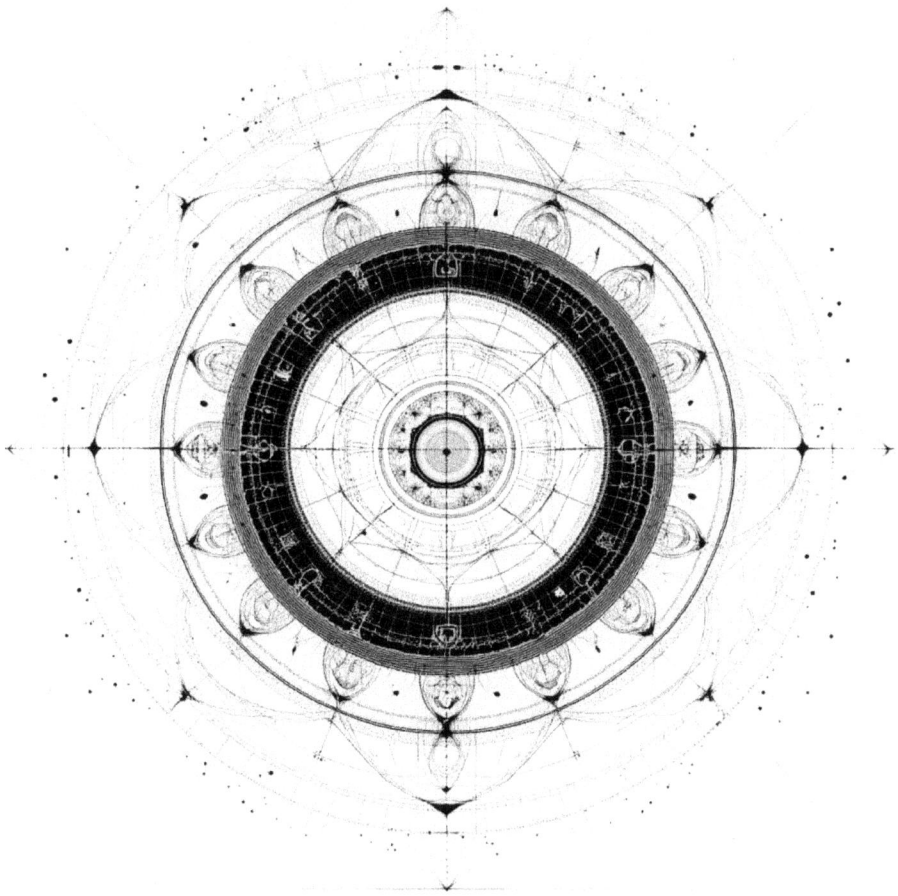

"To change the world for the better, you must begin by changing your own life. There is no other way."

~ **Seth**

CHAPTER 20

GOLDEN LIGHT HEALING
GETTING TO THE ROOT CAUSE OF ALL YOUR PAIN

By Joanne Figov, BA, Dip.V.Med, BTAA

MY STORY

My childhood in Cape Town was during the dying days of apartheid. The atmosphere of fear and desperation outside often mirrored my home life, which felt like a war zone.

Angry screams of my volatile mother filled the air. I learned to be quiet, and my voice was shut down. Left alone with my daydreams, I became aware of other worlds, other beings, which, as a child, gave me comfort.

At night, I often had dreams and visions which I didn't understand. I woke up hearing screams in my head from the township violence I had vicariously witnessed.

In the morning, I realized my dreams were reality as the impartial newsreaders told us that the brutal army infiltrated the African townships in the middle of the extreme cold of winter and destroyed the tin shanties. The screaming and voices in my head haunted me for years.

I was a sensitive child, and it was only when I became a young adult that I started understanding the feelings, visions, and dreams I experienced. It was a type of psychic phenomenon that continued throughout my life and eventually became a source of great help and understanding when I connected with the spirit world.

My father and I were very similar, and I loved sitting in his study, reading his many books on spiritualism, famous mediums, healing, and the paranormal. The sleeping prophet, Edgar Cayce, gripped my imagination. Those books brought me such joy to realize that there was more than this earthly realm.

Reading books on miracle healings felt like magic in my hands. Years later when I happily worked in my healing practice, I realized I was repeating the magic experienced in childhood.

This childhood magic is a powerful message for budding entrepreneurs!

What was your spark of passion or enthusiasm as a child or an adult? What dreams have you secretly nurtured in your heart and not put out into the world? What challenges have you overcome that changed and shifted you onto another path? Did you know that your inner healing and connecting to the passion of your childhood could be key to the growth of your dreams and career?

All my life I have been fascinated by the mysteries of the universe, consciousness, and energy, and how they all have a part to play in healing body, mind, and soul. I always learned, read, went to courses, and remained open and curious.

My early a-ha moment was in 1995 at one of the first Bowen technique seminars in the UK. I lived in the south of England, and it was there that I found my magic healing method!

As well as pain relief, realigning the body, releasing emotions and trauma from the tissues, the hands-on Bowen technique has a remarkable effect on the autonomic nervous system and resetting the relaxation response.

A student in class had a ten-year history of severe frozen shoulder due to an accident, and he couldn't move his arm further than a few inches from the side of his body. The teacher made a few simple Bowen moves on his shoulder.

We waited two minutes for the work to integrate. Then his arm floated easily up to his ear. Silence descended in the room. We were all stunned.

Holy Mackerel.

How did that happen?

I was hooked!

In that moment I knew this was what I would do with my life, to get these results to help others out of pain.

I started my Bowen practice, working with different ailments that people presented with. I relished the creative freedom in my clinic. It felt like a magical science laboratory as I learned, observed, and saw results with how people responded.

For a world seemingly overwhelmed by stress, I found Bowen to be a valuable tool.

Putting hands on the client's body felt like a holy act, touching not only the body but sensing a whole life.

There is so much more to explore here! I can't wait!

And yet, I was largely unaware of the huge stress within my own body. Looking back, I was in denial; my mind protected me from unconscious pain. I practiced yoga, ate nutritious food, exercised, and meditated. I thought I was fine.

How wrong I was!

In those early years in my clinic, I noticed a pattern in my clients of how the emotional cause of physical pain was trapped in the tissues, fascia, and cells of the body. As trapped energy of emotional pain was released from the body, the physical symptoms dramatically reduced.
The issues are in the tissues!

The physical and emotional issues are two sides of the same coin—wow!

A few years into my Bowen practice, the phone rang.

"Joanne, I'd love for you to come be a tutor," said Ossie. It was my Australian Bowen teacher, and he wanted me to help him establish the first Bowen Association in the UK.

That moment ignited a life-changing journey, allowing me to travel the world and teach this incredible technique, forging beautiful friendships along the way.

Soon after, I experienced one of my prophetic dreams. In it, I stood in the shadows of a room, observing my Bowen teacher, Ossie Rentsch, as he worked on a client lying on the treatment table. Suddenly, Ossie paused, tapped the person on the cheek, looked directly at me, and spoke three unforgettable words: "Ask the body!"

I woke up knowing another level of healing waited to be revealed.

I had no idea what to do, but felt directed by invisible forces. I put my hands on the client's body, closed my eyes, and waited.

Slowly, messages floated in. Into my head popped a mixture of the age when a client's trauma happened—words, images, knowing, and feelings about them.

As the invisible realms from childhood opened up in my healing practice, I felt the same sense of excitement as when I was young.

Embracing my intuition, my awareness expanded, and I merged deeper with the healing energy of Bowen and my spirit guides. I realized I was going beyond the technique into subtle realms of other possibilities.

My hands became a listening tool, revealing messages and emotions trapped in various areas of the body. Colors lit up in my mind's eye, directing me to areas of concern. I seemed to be shapeshifting as I merged with the client's body. I felt what they were feeling.

Past-life glimpses, other timelines, and ethereal beings appeared. There seemed no end to the extraordinary possibilities beyond the five senses. As I tuned in, layers of trauma revealed their secrets, and clients were guided toward a way to heal.

On occasion, deceased relatives and pet animals appeared with messages. Though I don't consider myself a medium, these insights appeared when clients were in desperate need, offering the healing specifically required that day. The results I witnessed showed me how healing can open doors to the spiritual dimension, the soul, and the interconnectedness of us all.

My client Suzi sat up after the end of her treatment, opened her eyes, and said, "I saw my soul."

She described her vision: "It is like a beautiful tapestry woven from this world and beyond, filled with love and guiding me to embrace myself fully."

My clients became my teachers.

I always wished to be a psychic medium, and it never happened. Now I realized my intuition opened up with my healing. I felt so grateful!

The fascination of the esoteric world never left me, and synchronicity brought the wisdom of the Tarot into my life, as well as a passion for flower essence healing. Both brought a whole new level of guidance for me and my clients.

The wonderful healing energy of flower remedies aided in peeling back layers of emotions and issues for clients and helped in identifying the root cause.

Fast forward 20 years, and I found myself once again visited by a timely prophetic dream. I noticed in my practice that there was a shift in energy, that people were more open and awake, desiring deeper change. An evolution in healing was happening.

In this dream, a person lay on my treatment table, and suddenly, I was enveloped in a brilliant flash of golden light. Descending, golden light beings gently touched the spine with DNA spirals, and a message came through:

This new therapy will be called Golden DNA, symbolizing the activation and elevation of DNA to a higher frequency.

This name resonated with me for a few years; then I was intuitively guided to simply change it to Golden Light Healing.

I started using Bowen Therapy and Golden Light Healing as two separate therapies, depending on the needs of clients.

Life was good. I felt I was living the dream—a lovely partner, clients flowing through my door, traveling the world, and inspiring students with this wonderful modality.

And then it stopped! Just like that.

I lost 15 years of my life! A sudden health crisis beginning in 2006 thrust me into the dark night of the soul.

Unbeknownst to me, emotional trauma had quietly built up inside me since I was a child. It was no coincidence that it was all locked within my neck, throat, and jaw area, the home of self-expression. It manifested physically in a condition known as dysphagia. Suddenly, I couldn't swallow food or drink, and for years, my doctors said, "It's in your head; there's nothing much that can be done."

I proved them wrong!

Finally, scans revealed the muscles of the lower part of my esophagus weren't working.

My confidence ebbed away. I stopped socializing. I couldn't go on dates. I was in constant pain with headaches, neck, and jaw discomfort. My teeth cracked with excess chewing and the pressure of trying to swallow.

Sometimes, damage to physical structure needs support. A holistic dentist specializing in jaw dysfunction provided me with an appliance to wear on my teeth at night. That and regular Bowen work gradually re-adjusted my jaw to the correct position essential for physical healing.

At the time, I was at the height of my Bowen career. I stopped going to conferences and interacting with colleagues. I felt a wretched failure, helping others and unable to help myself. I became a recluse and continued seeing clients. Little did they know they were keeping me going, that seeing them and giving treatments was the one constant giving me joy.

My special connection to spirit was lost in my raging sea of anger and frustration.

Why is this happening to me? Why can't I help myself?

When a psychologist family friend kindly said she would see me for a few sessions, I remember thinking:

I wonder what we are going to talk about?

We sat down; she looked at me and said, "Tell me about your childhood."

The world stopped. I couldn't breathe.

Something clicked inside my brain, and I heard a strange sound and wondered where it was coming from.

It was me!

I howled throughout the session and didn't even know why. Thus began the long journey back home to my body, myself.

There was no overnight miracle for me. Deep inner healing is painful. Nothing prepares you for that. Layers of trapped emotion, early trauma, past lives, negative self-beliefs, and a total lack of self-love took years of unraveling and understanding. My body and soul were sending me messages in the form of physical symptoms, and it got louder and louder until it exploded.

Our body truly is a reflection of our consciousness!

The root cause of my condition went back to those early years with my mother: fear and anxiety trapped in my little body and my voice being silenced. All of this quietly stored up for years around my jaw, neck, and throat area, waiting to implode.

There is usually a trigger to any explosion. Mine was the trauma of my long-term relationship dissolving in that same year, 2006. My body couldn't hold it together any longer and tipped over the edge. That's when my symptoms started. I disappeared into a dark void.

This new reality I found myself in was a prison of my own making. I was confused as to how I got to that point.

One afternoon, after exhausting myself with crying, I lay on the sofa and closed my eyes. As I lightly dozed, I felt the familiar feelings from childhood stirring, the invisible world of spirit comforting me and reminding me of the heavenly realms.

The golden light beings appeared. Peace descended upon me, and my heart overflowed with such intense love from their high frequency that I spontaneously cried tears of joy.

I opened my eyes, and, in that moment, I felt an energetic shift. Hope had returned!

On my office wall hangs a quote:

"In the midst of winter, I found there was, within me, an invincible summer."
~ Albert Camus

I started communicating with my body. My anger and emotional pain were so all-consuming that I disconnected. My body became my teacher. I became kinder to myself, a friend and not the enemy. My fascia and tissues gradually responded by softening, emotions were released, and my symptoms gradually improved. Lifelong patterns, suppressing my voice and holding me back, started lifting.

Practicing the difficult art of self-forgiveness and cultivating self-love became part of the journey home. That alone (with many other lessons) is something I added into my own life and work with clients. We often nurture others while neglecting our own needs.

Lockdown for COVID in 2020 was a pivotal part of my final recovery, pushing my progress to a miraculous 95%. Those months of doing 'nothing' was the time it took to finally heal my hyperactive nervous system, which I believe never had a long enough period of time to fully heal from childhood PTSD.

I became my own laboratory. The more my condition improved, the more I expanded energetically, and the more my business shifted and thrived. My awareness and connection to my soul essence became stronger.

We are so much more than a biological body. We are indeed spirit and energy and part of a magical cosmos.

My most profound turning point was while I was out at a restaurant with friends. For the first time in 15 years, I savored the simple act of eating, a gift we overlook and take for granted. As I took a bite and swallowed normally, a wave of gratitude washed over me, and I felt an overwhelming connection to something greater. In that moment, I looked up. Out of the corner of my eye, a beautiful golden light sparkled. I smiled and offered thanks to the invisible beings who guided me to this miraculous moment.

I would love to share a beautiful healing meditation that was given to me by the golden light beings. This is my gift to you.

THE TOOL

Listen to the full meditation on my website:
https://www.joannefigovhealing.com/golden-light-healing-meditation/

Find a comfortable position, sitting or lying down. Close your eyes. Take a few deep breaths, inhaling for a count of four and exhaling for a count of seven. Let each breath relax your body deeper.

Step away from the world's noise and distractions. Visualize your energy expanding, becoming vibrant and light, as if you were floating. Imagine a Golden Light above your head, a pulsating ball of warmth and comfort, gently descending towards you.

As the light reaches your crown, sense golden beings surrounding you, radiating love and peace. Your light-body is awakening, reconnecting with your soul family across dimensions and lifetimes. Allow the golden light to flow down your neck, spine, and body, filling you with warmth and love. It saturates every cell, bringing joy and healing.

Feel this light open your heart wide, filling you deeply. Allow it to travel down your legs, into your feet, grounding you to Earth. Your entire body vibrates with golden light, reconnecting you to your true essence through your awakening soul. This radiant soul is always with you, ready to bring healing, peace, and clarity.

Now, place your hands on any area of discomfort or tension. If there is no pain, put your hands on your heart. The healing light will address whatever is needed, physical, emotional, mental, or spiritual. As you rest your hands on the area, breathe in the Golden Light, feeling it flow into your hands. You may feel warmth or tingling as the healing energy activates.

Ask the area what it wishes to communicate. Be open to receiving insights, whether through colors, emotions, thoughts, or simply knowing. As this process unfolds, old energies may surface and release, making space for new healing.

Visualize your spine as a doorway opening to new energy, allowing the golden light spirals to activate specific areas.

Now, if you're ready and willing, say aloud:

"I willingly release from all the cells in my body and all timelines, that which no longer serves me. I release what holds me back from my true potential. I invite the golden light to heal me now."

Pause.

Then say aloud:

"I invoke the gift of the golden light. I allow it to flow through me, reaching the parts of me most in need. I relinquish all that no longer serves me. I embrace the gift of the golden light. I honor the power of the universe that surrounds me in Light."

Pause.

As your light body activates and your frequency rises, feel healing flood through you. Your aura expands in golden light, connecting you to all beings of the highest frequencies. We are all interconnected.

Feel your soul vibrating with golden light, trusting everything is in perfect alignment. Your soul rises into its magnificence, restoring balance and healing. When you're ready, begin to bring awareness back to the present. Know you can connect with this light anytime, simply by visualizing it within your heart. Gently move your fingers and toes, focus on your breath, and, when you're ready, open your eyes.

Joanne Figov, BA, Dip.V.Med, BTAA, is an intuitive healer with over 25 years of practicing and teaching the Bowen Technique worldwide and a founder member of the Bowen Association UK. She has a diploma in Vibrational Medicine and is the creator of a healing method called Golden Light Healing.

Her journey began with a BA degree in anthropology from the University of Cape Town and a diploma in psychiatric nursing, both enriching her understanding of a multifaceted approach to health and well-being.

By merging her intuitive wisdom with many healing modalities, including flower and light frequency essences, tarot soul coaching, past life readings, yoga, and trance healing, Joanne provides a unique approach to wellness. Her work addresses the physical, emotional, mental, and spiritual levels of being. Her healing sessions in person and online are individually tailored to release clients from physical and emotional pain and create shifts in consciousness. Joanne's passion is firstly to facilitate healing and then guide clients to tap into their intuitive guidance to access their soul's highest wisdom, for growth and transformation.

Joanne has been mentored by some of the world's top healers, mediums, and medical intuitives.

She has a full-time practice on the south coast of England as well as offering online sessions. See her website for monthly online groups, small group healing sessions, and programs.

When she's not working, you will find her walking by the sea, taking photographs for the joy of it, dancing to music, reading poetry aloud, and enjoying green tea in china teacups. Joanne would love to hear your story and support you on your path to wellness—reach out today!

"We are all walking each other home."
~ Ram Dass

Connect with Joanne:

Website: https://www.joannefigovhealing.com
Facebook: https://www.facebook.com/joannefigov
Instagram: https://www.instagram.com/joanne_figov_healing/
YouTube: https://www.youtube.com/channel/UCqRs_cSB2Qxva554nKleJog
Email: joannebowen8@gmail.com

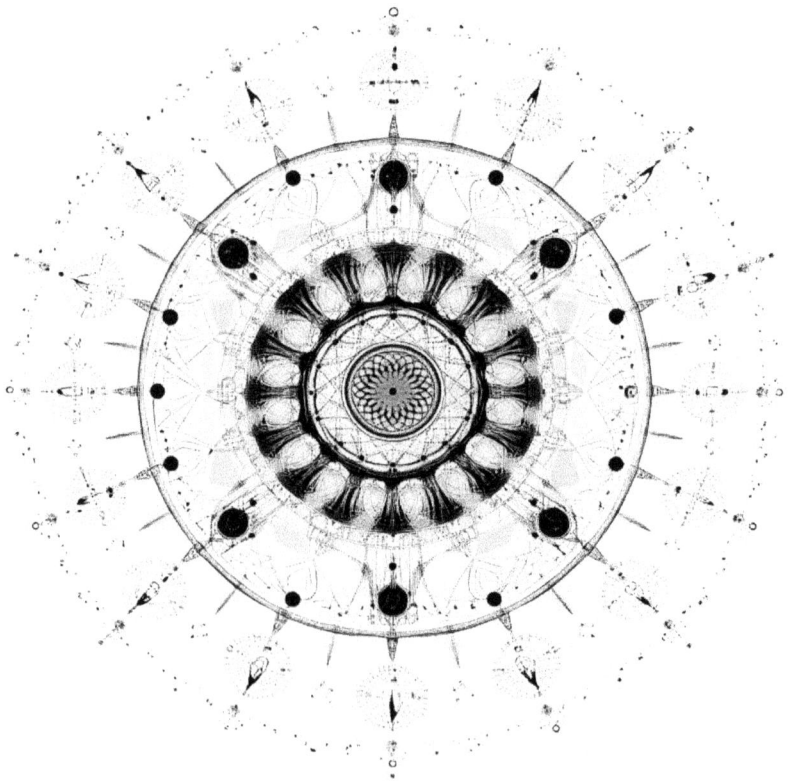

CHAPTER 21

STEP INTO YOUR POWER

Using Visualization to Navigate

Difficult Decisions

By L'Aura Montgomery Williams, BSBA, KRM

MY STORY

Anxiety tightened around my chest like a rubber band being stretched way too thin. Breathing was difficult, and my head pounded. Sleeping was out of the question.

Why was it so hard to make this decision?

It had been six years since the majestic mountains, the striking blue skies, the antelopes at play, and the clean, crisp air called me to move across the country to Colorado.

I first came to Colorado for a one-week work assignment as an East Coast media consultant in 2005. After standing in awe, looking at the incredible sunsets and amazing views of the Rocky Mountains, I flew home, gave away all my belongings, packed up my camping gear in my car, and headed west!

New beginnings, new people, new scenery! I can be anyone I want to be!

I always prided myself on listening to my intuition and acting on it with ease. People called me brave, but trusting my intuition never felt like a risk.

Driving to Colorado, the windows down and the song Free Bird blaring on

213

an endless loop, I repeated out loud to myself, "I have no idea how much goodness the Universe has in store for me!"

I felt my own personal power—the feeling which comes from trusting and taking such a big leap of faith. Free Bird became my theme song! I felt free and I was soaring.

I landed in an eclectic little hamlet at the base of Pikes Peak. I certainly saw why the snow capped 14,000' summit of Pikes Peak inspired Katherine Lee Bates to write America the Beautiful. It's truly a stunning backdrop for new beginnings.

I did not know a soul and had four boxes to my name with my history, altar, favorite books, and some clothes. I became a displaced East Coast media consultant in the mountains of Colorado, waiting on tables in a breakfast restaurant and loving every minute of it.

I embraced freedom, welcomed the not-knowing, and anticipated whatever it was the Universe had in store for me. I knew, as Esther Hicks says, "Everything is always working out for me."

These feelings of freedom weren't entirely new. During my 45 years, I made a lot of other big decisions easily: the decision to quit drinking alcohol when I turned 30, the decision to leave a failing marriage after 23 years, and the decision to give up my consulting practice and move to Colorado knowing no one. Trusting my intuition became second nature.

So how can I go from feeling free and empowered to being so anxious and unable to decide what to do?

Six months after my arrival in Colorado, I met Lane, a man who was to be my new husband. I loved his easy-flowing nature, desire for self-improvement, and trust in my intuition, as well as his own. He was and still is an incredible artist, custom-creating very fine gold and silver jewelry from an idea in his head. The only problem seemed to be his right brain is so dominant that he needed someone to help him run his solo business.

"I think you need me in your business," I boldly told him a few months into our dating.

"I think you're right," he said. He gave me 50% interest in his business, and a team was born.

Not only was it a business team, but a spiritual team!

"Lane is a right brain, and I'm a left brain, and together we make a whole brain," I was fond of saying to our customers.

A year later, we surprised ourselves by hiring our first employee who just happened to walk into our shop looking for a job, and the rest is history.

Fast forward five years: We have three stores and 14 employees. The only business plan we ever had was to walk through the doors that open. We welcomed each other's intuition and prospered doing so.

In those five years, walking through the doors that opened not only worked for us professionally but also personally—it allowed us to go see the Dalai Lama up close and personal, pivot our business during the housing crash, and become debt-free.

"Your stores are beautiful," our customers said. "I love how sparkly the diamonds and jewelry look under the glass," others commented. "You have done such a great job expanding your locations. I can't wait to see what you do next."

I loved the adulation. I felt accomplished. I felt important. Everything was working, and everything was working out!

"We need to close the new store," Lane said to me one afternoon.

What? Where was that coming from?

"We need to close the new store," he reiterated.

"I am not ready for that," I stated.

I didn't want to consider closing the new store. I was attached to the idea that I was winning! We succeeded at growing our business to a point we never imagined possible.

Summer fast approached, and the store was in a great location in a tourist town. We were only one year into a three-year lease and were profitable the first year. It made no sense to me.

The thing about intuition is that it makes no sense to the logical mind. Lane's intuition made no sense to me.

Days passed, and we continued running the business as usual; Lane didn't say much about it, but I saw him watching me. What is he sensing that I'm not seeing?

As I lay in bed that night, rolling over to catch the sinister glow of 4 a.m. on the clock radio, my mind was still confused about our conversation several days earlier.

Lane's words kept playing through my mind. *Maybe he's right. No, he isn't!*

We recruit reason as an ally of the ego to justify not listening to our inner voice, I thought, paraphrasing a line from one of my favorite books, *You Can Find Inner Peace*, by Mike George.

Maybe I stopped taking the time to listen to my inner voice. I was so involved in growing and running our business that I forgot to check in with it. I was so wrapped up in appearances and adulation.

Was my ego running the show? Was I using my ego to justify keeping the store open? These were questions I wasn't sure I wanted to answer yet.

However, I knew it was time to check in with my inner voice, the one that allowed me to feel so free and empowered. I needed to ask for some help— some guidance from my intuition.

"Honey, I can't sleep; I am going to go get in the hot tub," I mumbled to Lane. He kissed me on the cheek and continued snoring.

As I grabbed my fluffy bathrobe and slippers, I heard in my head: You need to close the new store.

But the new store has only been open a year, and we're successful. It showed a profit the first year!

I remember it was a Sunday morning and Mother's Day in 2012. I had the day off, but the new store was open on Sundays.

As I slipped into the hot tub and the warm water enveloped me, I realized how much stress I was under. *Is this what Lane is sensing?*

I realized that it hadn't seemed to matter to me that I was under a lot of stress. It didn't seem to matter that I gave away all the freedom and personal power I experienced when I moved to Colorado. I gave my freedom up for the accolades and the feeling of accomplishment. The stress and minutiae of managing and running three stores took its toll.

I never even stopped long enough to hear the small voice within telling me I needed to slow down, but Lane could see it.

So, it was time. Time to check in. Time to tune out all the noise in my monkey brain and ask the Universe to show me the best path for the highest good of all involved, something I had somehow forgotten to do.

If you just tune in, ask, and trust, you will know, I heard softly in my head. *Aha! My inner voice! It's still there.*

The gentle whirring sound of the hot tub and the delicate scent of the chilly Colorado spring air stilled my mind. I asked out loud, "What am I supposed to do?"

At that moment, I heard: Imagine each path and you will know.

I relaxed into the warm, bubbling water, closed my eyes, took several deep breaths of the cool, crisp early morning air, and visualized a scene in the woods with two paths diverging. *This reminds me of Robert Frost's poem.*

I saw myself taking the path on the right. I visualized myself closing the store. I envisioned not having to hire new people—no interviews, no reference or background checks. I imagined what it would feel like not having to worry about inventory but rather focusing simply on the other two operations. I envisioned moving the store manager to the downtown location. I felt so much peace and relief.

I quickly opened my eyes for a few seconds and pulled back from that vision. I paused, closed my eyes, and pictured taking the path on the left.

I imagined keeping the store open. I envisioned myself interviewing and hiring new people, keeping track of the inventory for three stores, and making sure to beef up security for the summer. I felt anxiety and my chest felt tense. It was hard to breathe.

My eyes flew open. The contrast was staggering. The clarity was empowering. I knew in that exact moment what I needed to do. No business analysis or advice from a peer could've given me a clearer knowing.

Oh wow! That was incredible. Thank you, Spirit. Thank you, Universe. I am so grateful!

I got out of the hot tub, woke up my still-dozing husband and declared, "You were right, we do need to close the new store." He smiled and gave me a kiss on the cheek, and went back to sleep.

That morning, after coffee, we drove to the new store and informed our store manager of the plans. I wasn't worried about what other people would think or that I would be seen as a "failure." It felt so freeing and empowering and right. I felt inspired!

We implemented the closing, and the landlord was gracious and assured us she'd be able to rent the highly prized location. "You don't need to worry about the lease," she said. We consolidated our inventory and employees into two locations.

We didn't know where this decision would lead, but we trusted it was the right thing to do, the next step on our journey, inspired action.

A few months later, a once-in-a-lifetime opportunity became available to us to purchase a retail space and move one of our other locations out of a rental space. This opportunity wouldn't have become available to us if we hadn't closed that store. Paying rent at three locations would've been too much financial liability to qualify for the mortgage.

Using the same principles of visualization, intuition, and inspired action, our new building would become our only store location during COVID. We integrated all of our inventory and employees under one roof. We believe consolidating is what allowed us to stay profitable and in business during the pandemic.

Currently, we're content. One store is perfect. We're happy and at peace!

Additionally, all this helped me realize that I didn't need to have three stores to feel successful. I still have to check on my ego—that's a lifetime commitment!

The feeling of accomplishment is now more about how I feel inside. Of course, compliments are still wonderful, but I don't have to prove anything to myself or anyone else. I just want to feel peace of mind and personal freedom.

Most recently, visualization and intuition have allowed me to move away from the jewelry business to follow my calling and divine purpose as a healer and high-vibe coach. It's another leap of faith, and I'm excited!

THE TOOL

Creative visualization and imagination can be incredible tools for clarity to navigate difficult decisions and point us in the right direction!

Once we feel inspired and know which path to take, we need to act in a timely manner. If we drag our feet it sets us up to give away our personal power and we end up living a life by default instead of creating an inspired and magical life by design.

Living an extraordinary life involves jumping in with both feet, trusting your spirit, and acting upon it. It also involves being willing to let go of things that no longer serve us and checking in with our higher self.

The Steps

Step One: Be willing.

Be willing is a huge two-word statement. What am I willing to let go of? What is no longer serving me? What am I willing to look at? What if someone else is right? What if someone else is seeing something I am not seeing?

Be willing to be honest with yourself.

Step Two: Ask for guidance.

I have used this method for both personal and business decisions. Sometimes I shout out loud; sometimes, I whisper it to myself, and other times, it's just a thought in my head.

"What am I supposed to do?" "Please help me decide what the best option is."

Simply by asking the question I have had insights and answers that have changed the course of my life.

Just ask!

Step three: Be still.

Find a quiet place, take a deep breath—sigh out loud, and be in an open and receptive state of mind. Ask your ego to step aside.

Step four: Expect, connect, and receive.

Knowing that the answer will come to you is a great advantage. Close your eyes and visualize your options. Pick one of your options and imagine following that decision in as much detail as possible. Imagine the sights, the people, the possible outcome. Notice how you are feeling. Immerse yourself in those feelings.

When the journey in your mind feels complete, pull back from that space mentally, and open your eyes briefly to ground yourself in your surroundings. Now close your eyes again and do the same visualization with your other option or options. Imagine the sights and people involved in as much detail as possible. Notice how you're feeling and immerse yourself in your feelings.

After this step, you'll probably have a clear answer to which path you want to pursue.

If things are still not clear, do not make a decision yet. Do something fun, take a walk in nature, and become present. You can try again another day. Return to Step One.

Step five: Express gratitude!

Thank you, thank you, thank you! I am so grateful!

Step six: Act on your decision.

The quicker you can take steps to implement the decision you made, the better. Acting on your intuition requires trust and commitment. If you don't act right away, your ego and monkey mind may chime in and make it more difficult!

Conclusion:

By using the creative power of the mind, we can receive clarity, healing, peace of mind, connection, personal power, and joy.

You can also use this method for small everyday decisions, like where to go for lunch today or what to write about in your next blog. You do not have to start out with big, life-altering decisions.

Take a deep breath, close your eyes, determine your options, visualize each option, "feel your vibes," thank the Universe/Source, act on it, practice, and repeat.

After a few times, it becomes second nature and is the gateway to stepping into your power and having a magical life by design.

Enjoy!

L'Aura Montgomery Williams, BSBA, KRM, is the founder of Mojo Reiki and co-owner of Lane Mitchell Jewelers. She holds a Bachelor's Degree in Business Administration and attended classes at Lancaster Theological Seminary, working towards her Master's degree in Religion.

In the early 1990's, L'Aura left a short-lived stint in corporate America to pursue her passion in spiritual activism in the field of equal rights for GLBT (gay, lesbian, bisexual, and transgender) people.

She became an organizer and media consultant to national non-profits with an emphasis in spiritual gay rights activism.

During this time, she oversaw dozens of civil disobediences at national church conventions to protest their discriminatory practices against GLBT people, including a direct action at the Vatican in Rome and at Focus on the Family in Colorado Springs.

L'Aura is known by her peers as a passionate, tenacious, and intuitive seeker who acts on her intuition and pursues her passions with zeal.

In 2005, she followed her call to Manitou Springs, CO, where she met Lane, a master jeweler. Together they grew Lane Mitchell Jewelers.

During COVID, L'Aura decided to investigate expanding her intuitive nature and spiritual roots by taking classes in reiki, shamanism, and psychic development.

She is now a White Light Reiki Master, Usui Reiki Ryoho Holy Fire® III Reiki Master, Karuna® Reiki Master, Shamanic Reiki Practitioner, Animal Reiki Practitioner, Animal Communicator, Sound Healing Practitioner, and High Vibe Coach.

Her business, Mojo Reiki, is a form of energy healing that combines reiki, meditation, relaxation, sound healing, and shamanic practices to help others tap into a higher vibration to promote healing, empowerment, transformation, and inspired action.

Connect with L'Aura:

Mojo Reiki:
Email: mojoreiki@gmail.com
Website: https://mojoreiki.com
Blue Sky: https://bsky.app/profile/mojoreiki.bsky.social

Lane Mitchell Jewelers:
Website: https://lanemitchelljewelers.com

Additional bio:

https://lgbtqreligiousarchives.org/profiles/laura-montgomery-rutt-williams

"Wonder is the beginning of wisdom."

~ **Socrates**

CHAPTER 22

THE "WHAT IF?" PRINCIPLE

5 Key Questions to Uplevel Your Business

By Donnabelle Casis

MY STORY

I'm an out-of-the-box thinker, but that wasn't always the case growing up. When I emigrated to the US from the Philippines as a young child, I was always told to blend in, to disappear in a way—acclimate so no one would notice a difference.

It was the '70s. My mother took my older sister and me from Manila to Seattle. After a tumultuous three-year marriage, my parents divorced. My mother believed it was best for us to move in with our extended family in the US.

My great-grandmother and I sat at the round kitchen table one early morning. It was covered with a vinyl, yellow, and brown floral tablecloth. The sun started to rise and I heard the birds outside the window, chirping and singing to welcome the day. I yawned as she handed me a small plate with two pieces of buttered toast cut diagonally. Next to the plate was a little taza (teacup) with diluted instant coffee and cream. Yes, I was a child who enjoyed coffee!

Ang sarap isawsaw ang tostadong tinapay sa kape para matikman ang lasa ng tinapay na tinubog sa kapeng galing sa Java at higupin ang masarap na pinagsawsawan.

How I loved dipping my toast triangles into the coffee, tasting the java-soaked bread, then slurping the buttery liquid.

You need to learn English," my great-grandmother remarked. "Stop speaking Tagalog or you won't make any friends," she chided.

That statement made such a profound impression on me that I completely lost my native tongue. I dressed like everyone, ate the same foods, and acted just like my peers. It worked for a while, but I felt like an imposter, hiding a part of me that wanted to express itself.

Creativity Cures What Ails You

I loved to doodle and make drawings when I was a kid.

I studied fine art, majoring in painting at college. I waited tables during the weekends to pay for tuition. My major was originally graphic design.

"You need to major in something that makes money so you can get a job," my mother and stepfather admonished.

When I held a paintbrush for the first time, I knew I found my muse. The scratchy sound the bristles made when they touched the canvas sent tingles up my spine. The brush felt like an extension of my hand as it swirled the paint around.

There was no turning back.

Earning my bachelor's and master's degrees in painting showed me ways I could express all aspects of myself through creativity.

A Bump in the Road

Well, two bumps, actually. After an incredible start to a career, exhibiting my artwork nationally and internationally, getting represented by a Seattle art gallery, and teaching art at the college level, I got married and gave birth to fraternal twin boys.

My professional art life took a big, long pause—seven years, in fact. Although I loved being a new mother, I longed for some creative time that didn't require a lot of head space. I was too exhausted to make the conceptual work I was used to making.

My artwork is informed by extensive research about markers of identity (tribal tattoos and textiles, societal structures, etc.). At one point, I studied chainmail patterns and the specific designs used for certain purposes, such as for warfare or decoration. I also studied various forms of adornment, like jewelry.

What if I made jewelry?

I like working with my hands. When the boys were napping, I managed to learn how to make enamel jewelry (with a kiln, copper, and powders) and taught myself how to print my drawings onto the fired glass surfaces. These drawings were more organic forms inspired by plants and flowers. I'm a Gemini, and I like things in twos (just like my babies!). So, I made the jewelry double-sided so you could have two options: wear a pattern with my art on one side or flip it over to wear a contrasting solid color.

I gave a few pieces as gifts for friends. The overwhelming response was: "You should sell these!" Thus, my first business, donnabelle.designs was born. For five years I sold my jewelry line through several boutiques, a museum shop, and indie craft fairs. Making jewelry gave me an outlet to create things in a limited amount of time and brought in some unexpected and welcomed income.

Tennis Anyone?

As my sons got older and more independent, I spent more time in the studio and had extra time to play tennis. We are a tennis family. One of my sons plays for his college team. I'm a tennis pro wanna-be.

As if.

I played almost ten times a week. I was a tennis maniac! After a hand injury and surgery, my tennis plans came to a grinding halt. My need to exercise and move was paramount, so I attended barre classes (think ballet training) where I spent most of the time standing near a handrail or lying down on the floor, and definitely not using my hands so much.

Staring at yourself in a wall-length mirror for sixty minutes is no picnic.
I didn't like what was available for athletic wear. I figured, if I have to look at myself in the mirror 240 minutes a week I could at least have decent clothes to stare at.

What if I made my own athleisure wear?

I took some images from older paintings I liked and transferred them onto leggings, skirts, shorts, tanks, bags, scarves, and other accessories. I wore some of them to barre class, where everyone said, "Where did you get those? You should sell them!" A museum shop and a boutique sold my athleisurewear line, plus I sold items directly to consumers on my donnabelle.designs website.

After the economic crash and the COVID pandemic hit, all sales moved to my online shop. The athleisure wear was made to order by a company with environmentally friendly production processes and ethical work practices. They also shipped the items to the client. Donnabelle.designs practically ran itself. And, by that time, I stopped making enamel jewelry to focus more time on my first passion, painting.

Is That You, Spirit?

Rewind to when I was six years old. Another aspect that made me unique, aside from being an artist, was that I could see and feel Spirit around me. I told my mother about what was happening, and she said, "That's nice, honey. Now go play outside."

I was raised Roman Catholic, and we all went to church on Sundays and holy days. The Philippine side of me knew about shamans, healers, and mystics. So, my family wasn't surprised about what I experienced but also wasn't that supportive. I didn't interact much with the spirits. I just watched and observed.

The first time I encountered and engaged with a spirit entity was when I lived in a beautiful Victorian house during my senior year of college. My roommates and I knew the house was haunted before we moved in. Other artist friends who lived there prior told us. We didn't care. We couldn't pass up living in this gorgeous place not far from campus.

My experience with this dark energy was quite terrifying and dramatic. Whatever composed this blacker-than-black mist that came into my room and whispered into my ear was not friendly. Unfortunately, I had no spiritual mentors at the time, and I didn't know what was happening or what to do. I decided then and there that I wanted no part of it. I shut down my "gifts" for almost thirty years.

My intuitive abilities came back unexpectedly after a somatic bodywork therapy session to treat some tennis sprains. As the energy practitioner worked on me I felt something equivalent to a sonic boom move throughout my entire body. I could sense the quantum field when I looked at my hands, which looked like 1,000 hands moving in unison. Soon afterward, my extra-sensory perceptions kicked into high gear. It was as if all the built-up psychic energy from nearly three decades wanted to spill out all at once. I could see, feel, and know things so clearly and easily. I also discovered I was a medium.

I honed my abilities with several internationally renowned spiritual teachers and mentors. I felt guided to learn trance mediumship (my paternal grandfather was a trance healer and channel) and Reiki healing.

I am now a certified evidential and trance medium, and a Reiki Master and teacher. I started my second business, Sonorous Light, LLC, to share my gifts and offer paths to healing. I'll explain where the name came from later.

True Colors

I'm still a professional artist and compelled to put a unique, creative twist on whatever I do. The few psychic mediums in my area offered typical industry-standard services and readings. Aura photography was available somewhere about an hour away. I wanted to provide something novel. One of my gifts is the ability to see color auras.

What if I made aura drawings for psychic readings?

What if I used color ribbons as a divination tool?

I called them psychic auracle readings. My favorite part during a session is when the client actively participates in the process. They set an intention about a particular concern and choose three ribbons from a bag of many colored strands. Each ribbon represented the current situation, the hindrance, and the outcome.

Adding psychic auracle readings was a game-changer. They are now as equally requested as my mediumship readings and Reiki healing sessions.

Sounds Good

My interest in sound goes back to high school. I loved music and noticed how different songs resonated within my body and helped my mood. In college, I took an instrument-building class to satisfy a sculpture requirement. I made hand-built percussion instruments, rain sticks, shekeres, and kalimbas.

Fast forward to a few years ago. After attending a sound bath meditation and being immersed in harmonious frequencies and vibrations, I knew I wanted to learn how to do that for myself and others. Little did I know that the instruments I made over thirty years ago would become tools I now use today in my sound therapy practice! My soul knew where I was headed before I did.

I noticed sound baths were being offered at yoga studios and halls. The artist in me kicked in and started brainstorming.

*What if I held sound baths at art venues? Who doesn't want to be surrounded by art and architecture **and** be immersed in healing sounds?*

Since I was also an arts radio host who spotlighted area artists and arts organizations, I was connected to many museum and gallery curators and administrators. I contacted several venues I thought had conducive spaces for sound baths. My approach involved pitching the event as a wellness service for their audience while providing an access point for potential new visitors to come to the venue.

I received an immediate response from a small historical museum twenty minutes away. It had a beautiful music room which used to house a collection of instruments from all over the world. The classical columns and vaulted ceilings encased a room built specifically for music concerts. The acoustics were sublime! *Can someone pinch me?* This place was a dream.

The room was on the main floor with tall windows overlooking the topiary gardens. The staff were so friendly and even helped to market the event. They even provided someone to check in attendees at the door. It was part of the agreement we split the proceeds 70/30. I now hold sound bath meditations once a month with sold-out to nearly-sold-out attendance.

Sound (thus the Sonorous part of Sonorous Light) is also something I incorporate into my Reiki sessions. I play crystal singing bowls to ground the space before the client session, and I use tuning forks at the end of the session to balance particular areas of the client's bio-magnetic energy field.

When thinking about offerings for my businesses, I always find ways to make my services unique to my strengths.

THE TOOL

So, what is the "What If?" principle? It's a way to position your business in new and distinctive ways by asking exploratory questions. Instead of employing cookie-cutter approaches to setting up your business, this principle helps you discover ways to make your offerings stand out and appeal to more clients.

Take Stock

Before you begin, take a moment to pause and get centered. Do some deep breathing exercises or a short meditation. Prepare yourself to be fully present and intentional with these exercises.

KEY QUESTION #1: What brings you Joy (yes, capital J)?

When we are happy doing what we do, abundance and prosperity flow freely to us. We attract high vibrational feelings and energies, fueling our passion and fortifying our purpose.

Is it the people you work with? The community? Is it the space you work in? Is it the work you do? What's the most fun thing you've done in your practice? These questions help give you a sense of what gets you out of bed and back to your work. They also help you remember why you started your business in the first place. When you feel Joy, that energy emanates from you and your business. Happy clients become great advocates for you! Even if they can't access it right away, working with you will make them feel and know joy is possible.

KEY QUESTION #2: What makes you YOU?

No two snowflakes are alike. That's the same for humans, even identical twins. The variances can be great or small. Each experience in your life made you who you are today.

How would you describe yourself to a total stranger? What are you proud of? What are your hopes, dreams, and interests? Write twenty things down that no one knows about you. Don't forget the quirky and even embarrassing parts of yourself. Being vulnerable is a superpower. It shows you are human and not a robot. No one wants healing from a robot. This list will remind you how special you are!

KEY QUESTION #3: What/who inspires you and why?

in·spi·ra·tion: the process of being mentally stimulated to do or feel something, especially to do something creative.

You are a creator! You learned or honed a skill and started a business. That takes courage, passion, and gumption.

When we see or experience something or someone that moves us, we feel deeply and are touched by grace. What is that essence that motivates you? How can your business impart that feeling to a client?

I designed my business cards as a fifty-crystal oracle deck. I love crystals and work with these allies in my spiritual practice. Each card has a beautiful photograph of a particular crystal, its name, healing properties and uses, and an affirmation. After a sound bath or reading, I invite the client to set an intention and choose a healing crystal message from a selection of my business cards spread face down. Nine times out of ten, the crystal card resonates deeply with the client. They get to keep the card as a reminder, and a QR code on it leads to my website and contact information.

Truth be told, this is not an original idea. I wish I was the brilliant one who thought of it first!

A breathwork practitioner inspired me. She created a playing card-sized deck as business cards. Each card had a word on the back. She had me pick a card. I got DIVINE. Of course, I kept it! The front of her business card included all her contact information. I decided I wasn't as clever to think of twenty distinctive words, so I chose something I loved: crystals. Her card is still on my altar in my studio. My clients like to collect different crystal cards from every visit. It's a win-win.

KEY QUESTION #4: What makes your business unique?

We all think our businesses are special. But how special? Do a Google search for ten businesses near you that may be similar to yours.

- Do you offer the same things? If so, what?
- Do you offer these services in the same way or differently? How?
- Do you offer other things? If so, what?

Finding a niche can help you attract your ideal clients. Even something as simple as an effective tagline under your business name can draw a future client's attention. Also, if you are a patron of another kind of business, what makes you come back for more?

KEY QUESTION #5: How does your business bring out all the parts of you that you love?

You came into this world to share your light. Your journey matters because it led you to create this endeavor. Future clients want to know your story and how you got inspired to do what you do. Your business is the gateway to all the ways you identify with the world and how you make it a better place to be in. Shine on!

Donnabelle Casis is the Owner of Sonorous Light, LLC, and donnabelle. designs. She is a certified evidential and trance medium, Usui and Karuna Reiki Master and Teacher, sound practitioner, and spiritual development mentor. Her podcast, "To Hum is Human," highlights conversations about tuning into our inner wisdom to express our passionate purpose.

Donnabelle earned her MFA at the University of Washington, where she taught as an adjunct instructor for several years. She is a curator and hosts an arts radio show called ArtBeat Report on WHMP in Northampton, Massachusetts. Donnabelle also founded and produced an annual, one-night arts street festival, Florence Night Out, for seven years. She has exhibited her work nationally and internationally, including at the Wing Luke Museum, Museum of History and Industry, Albany International Airport, TurnPark Artspace, PULP, Tacoma Art Museum, and Newport Art Museum, among others. She has received numerous awards and grants, including the Neddy Artist Fellowship for Painting granted by the Behnke Foundation and grants from the Northampton Arts Council/ Massachusetts Cultural Council. Her artwork is included in several public and private collections.

Donnabelle felt called to serve others after she gave her first mediumship reading. She discovered she could help heal both the physical and spiritual realms. Through her teaching, Donnabelle inspires others to access the power within themselves to align with their soul's purpose. She believes everyone embodies a divine light that can illuminate the world.

Connect with Donnabelle:

Website: https://www.sonorouslight.com
https://donnabelledesigns.com/about
https://donnabellecasis.com
Facebook: https://www.facebook.com/sonorous.light

https://www.facebook.com/profile.php?id=100063452108864
https://www.facebook.com/donnabelle.casis
Instagram: https://www.instagram.com/sonorous.light555
https://www.instagram.com/donnabelle.designs
https://www.instagram.com/thisisdbc
LinkTree: https://linktr.ee/donnabellecasis

CLOSING CHAPTER

Trusting the Path Ahead

By Deb DeCelle, Educational Medium and Mentor

As we reach the final pages of this journey together, I want to take a moment to acknowledge the incredible transformation that lies within you. You've already begun to uncover a deeper connection to your intuitive gifts, and now, it's time to step boldly into your soul-driven success.

Throughout this book, we've explored the powerful intersection between intuition and entrepreneurship. You've learned how to listen to the quiet whispers of your inner knowing and how to use that wisdom to guide your business decisions, your growth, and your path forward. By now, you may have already experienced shifts in how you show up in the world—whether in your work, relationships, or mindset. If so, know this: what you're experiencing is just the beginning.

The path of the intuitive entrepreneur is not always linear, and it's certainly not without its challenges. However, the beauty of this path is that when you allow your intuition to lead you, even the obstacles become growth opportunities. Your soul knows the way, and as you continue to cultivate this connection, you will find yourself aligning more deeply with the very purpose you are here to fulfill.

Trust in Your Inner Compass

As you enter the next phase of your entrepreneurial journey, I encourage you to trust the inner compass that has always been there, quietly guiding you. Whether your intuition speaks through a gut feeling, a vivid dream, or a soft whisper in your ear, know that these messages are not random. They are the breadcrumbs leading you to the life and business you are meant to create. Trust them. Honor them.

There will be times when the world around you feels uncertain or when external pressures push you to make decisions that don't resonate with your soul. In these moments, remember that you are your greatest source of wisdom. Take a step back, quiet your mind, and reconnect with your inner truth. Trust that when you are aligned with your soul's purpose, the universe will conspire to support you in ways you cannot yet imagine.

Embrace the Expansion of Your Gifts

In this book, we've only begun to scratch the surface of what's possible when you align your intuition with your entrepreneurial vision. You are not only an entrepreneur; you are a soul-led visionary with the power to create a profound impact in the world. Your intuitive gifts are expanding, and with each step you take, you'll discover new ways to integrate these abilities into your work and your life.

As you continue on this path, I invite you to remain open to the endless possibilities that lie ahead. Trust that your intuition will guide you to opportunities, partnerships, and ideas that will propel you forward. Don't be afraid to dream big and take bold action. You have the power to create the life and business that reflects your deepest desires and highest potential.

Your Soul-Driven Success Awaits

Success, as we've explored, is not defined by external measures alone. It's about alignment, authenticity, and the fulfillment that comes from doing what you love in a way that serves others. Your success is already unfolding in ways you may not yet fully see. The seeds you've planted by connecting with your intuition are growing, and soon, they will bloom into something extraordinary. I want to remind you that there is no one else like you. Your unique combination of gifts, experiences, and insights is your superpower in the world of entrepreneurship. Embrace it fully, and trust that the world needs exactly what you have to offer. Your intuition is your guiding star; let it lead you as you step into the greatness you are destined for.

A Call to Action: The Time is Now

Now is the time to take action. Now is the time to step into your intuitive power and trust in the infinite possibilities before you. The world needs your unique energy, and as you begin to live and work from this soul-aligned place, you'll find that everything you need is already within you.

You've spent the last chapters diving into your intuition and uncovering the tools to align it with your entrepreneurial vision. Now, it's time to put them into practice. Take that first step, trust the process, and know that as you move forward, you are supported, guided, and loved by the universe. The time is now for you to create a business, a life, and a world that reflects your true soul's calling.

"The future belongs to those who believe in
the power of their dreams."

~ **Eleanor Roosevelt**

ACKNOWLEDGEMENTS

With Gratitude

Writing this book has been a journey of intuition, trust, and alignment, and I am deeply grateful for those who have supported and inspired me along the way.

To Rich Siek, Davia Boyle, Joli Dame, Mike Rossi, Neal Roylance, Siobhan LeBlanc, Jimmy Santarcangelo, and Leslie Depew thank you for saying yes. Your belief in me and support for this project from the moment I asked made this possible.

To my co-authors and collaborators, your wisdom, authenticity, and dedication to this work make this book a beacon for those who seek deeper connection and soul-driven success. I am so incredibly grateful to be with each and every one of you on this journey. Thank you for saying yes to YOU and for being brave healers who are willing to share brave words with the world! You are my dream team!

To Julie Speetjens (aka Jules), thank you for being the definition of a soul sister. Your loyalty, wisdom, and willingness to jump in when I needed you most made all the difference. This project simply wouldn't have succeeded without you.

To Atlantis Wolf, thank you for being an invaluable writing resource to our team. Thank you for the wisdom you carry deep in your soul, which empowers others to find peace within the stormiest of waters.

To Camy Kennedy, thank you for helping me realize that I could be terrified, imperfect, bawling my eyes out, and still take aligned action. Thank you for helping me realize that I am safe, and enough, exactly how I am.

To Joanne Figov, thank you for the wonderful healing energy and love that I desperately needed at the end of this project.

To Laura Bailey, thank you for your magic. It has kept me whole even when I felt as if I was hanging by a thread. Even when I didn't believe in myself, your belief in me has carried me through more times than you can imagine.

To Shannon Mitchell, thank you for truly understanding my chaos at the soul level and for helping me reframe things when I'm uncertain. Thank you for sharing your wisdom not only with me but also with my family. You're one of us now.

To the brilliant artist Davide De Angelis, whose visionary work has brought this book to a completely different level. Having collaborated with the legendary David Bowie, Davide is a masterful creator and a true intuitive entrepreneur, embodying the very essence of this book's message. My friend, there's a bit of the Starman himself in your work, and it's absolutely brilliant! Your artistry and insight inspire, thank you for sharing your gifts with this project and the world!

To Laura Di Franco and the Brave Healer Team for bringing this project to life. I deeply appreciate your dedication, vision, and commitment to helping authors share their voices with the world. The countless hours spent reviewing, editing, and perfecting every detail are what make you so much more than "just" a publisher. I have grown in many unexpected ways throughout this project and am a better me because of it. Your big visions inspire me.

To my family, friends, and those who have become family, especially my beloved husband **Heath, Tim, Matt, Sky, Bri, Shar, Joli, Dave, Kristy, Kath, Nick, Judy, Rich and his beloved Andrea, Mom K., Leanne, Stacy, Chrissy, Mary, and Bryan** your encouragement, belief, and unwavering support have meant everything. Thank you for walking this path with me, for lifting me up in moments of doubt, and for celebrating every success along the way. Thank you for keeping me sane (even on commute chats) and reminding me to get out of my mind and into my magic! You are all precious to me!

To my clients and students, you are my greatest inspiration, especially **Peggy Rehm, Laura Lembke Bens, Leslie Depew, Kim Harte Baccoli, and Kate Luscombe**. Your courage, breakthroughs, and willingness to embrace your intuitive power remind me why this work matters. It is an honor to witness your growth and transformation.

To Kelly Daughtery, thank you for choosing me to write on *The Grief Experience, Tools for Acceptance, Resilience, and Connection*. Your project gave me the courage to create my own as a lead author. Thank you for being my number one resource for grieving clients and for holding space for me in my seasons of grief last year.

To Cheri Davies, thank you for being the extra eyes I needed to get my word count down and for your advice when I needed it most. It means more than you'll ever know.

To Rebecca "TT" Rainstrom, thank you for encouraging me and sharing laughter. Your smile lights up the world and makes it a better place.

To the unseen forces, guides, guardians, and loved ones in Spirit, thank you for whispering, nudging, and aligning synchronicities that make the impossible possible, especially **Mom, Dad, Eleanor, and Drake**.

And finally, thank you, **the reader**, for being here, open, and trusting yourself enough to embark on this journey. May these pages help you step into your intuitive power, knowing that success is not just about strategy but about alignment, purpose, and divine flow.

With love and gratitude,
Deb xo

Unlock your intuitive potential and embrace your soul's purpose! Deb's guidance will empower you to make aligned decisions, live authentically, and create the life, and business, you desire. Join her on your very own transformative journey. Your intuition is waiting to lead you to success! Connect with Deb and schedule your complimentary 1:1 mentoring consult here!

Email me at deb@debdecelle.com or visit my

Website at https://www.debdecelle.com